THE *loss* BOX

JUDY LEE

THE *loss* BOX

HOW TO ACCEPT LOSS IN OUR LIVES

Matador
9 Priory Business Park
Kibworth Beauchamp
Leicestershire LE8 0RX, UK
Tel: (+44) 116 279 2299
Fax: (+44) 116 279 2277
Email: books@troubador.co.uk
Web: www.troubador.co.uk/matador

ISBN 978 1783061 495

British Library Cataloguing in Publication Data.
A catalogue record for this book is available from the British Library.

Typeset in Aldine401 BT Roman by Troubador Publishing Ltd
Printed and bound in the UK by TJ International, Padstow, Cornwall

Matador is an imprint of Troubador Publishing Ltd

This book is dedicated to the tenacity and endurance of the human spirit.
(And to Joe who insisted I write a book, and to Sue who told me I would.)

CONTENTS

FOREWORD

Loss is earthed in our intimate selves, what is currently described as the soul. It is something all of us experience, and is part of the reality of impermanence. Loss is always a point of beginning as much as it is an end, a releasing as much as a mourning.

Loss can be one of the greatest teachers of love, if we find the courage to embrace it. Ultimately, loss reveals the need for forgiveness, the need to forgive ourselves and others, and perhaps it also illuminates what has and is causing us pain.

In one life we lose so many things. To a certain degree we all lose our innocence, even if this is a gradual unfolding. The rigours of life make it likely that there have been periods when we have lost trust, hope, or vigour. We may have lost friendships, or dreams. Unless we can embrace and understand the very nature of our feelings we will never be able to understand what we have lost. Until we are able to understand what we have lost we will only partially be able to appreciate what we have gained as a result of such loss. It is, however, when we hold on to our feelings of loss that they come, to a certain extent, to define our being. We are caught in the grip of a constant grieving.

We lose our faith in justice when we have been treated unjustly. We lose our trust in others when our trust has been betrayed. But hanging on to those deep feelings and deep hurts can only embitter us. The pain of that experience roots into the shadow of our souls, our being.

Soul is being, the ground of being. It is not something singular although we may experience it as such. Soul is the shared song of existence; it is our own melody, but it sits within a symphony and it can only be known through the mirror of all other life. Our souls, therefore, are both one and many at the same time.

Loss is not always personal, the loss that others experience speaks to us profoundly if we are brave enough to let it do so, brave enough to let it in. If we are to move forward as a species, to create a reality where we recognise the immense healing potential that loss always presents, then we will need to know loss in all its forms and intensities and understand it as the teacher that it always is.

Peter Owen-Jones, Anglican priest, author and broadcaster.

INTRODUCTION

You cannot stop the birds of sorrow from landing on your shoulder,
but you can prevent them nesting in your hair.

Chinese proverb

Some years ago, on the spur of the moment, I underwent aura imaging at a psychic fair. I did it purely out of curiosity, but found the results fascinating.

The resulting picture showed, amongst other things, a large expanse of colour across my head, chest and solar plexus. The photographer explained this was grief I was carrying with me and suggested I took the findings seriously.

Whether or not I, or you, believe in aura imaging is academic; what I heard that day struck a chord with me and I knew what she said was right. The knowledge of this underlying sorrow was most likely there all along in my subconscious, but her words brought this truth to the surface and I could no longer ignore it. Where had this sadness come from and what could I do about it?

I had had my ups and downs like most people, but at that time I had not lost people close to me through death. I earned enough to pay the bills, I had three loving children and I was blessed with good friends, so most of my days had a healthy dose of warmth and laughter. It wasn't perfect but I had a good life.

I am not sure when it occurred to me that such pain might stem from accumulated loss which had gone unrecognised, but when it did I felt a gradual sense both of relief and release, and I was determined to find a way of consciously letting go and moving on.

I live in the centre of a small town which has a bypass. During the day when there is bustle and the noise of life all around, I am unaware of the passing traffic. At night, however, when the busyness calms down, there it is, a continuous background hum from the distant road.

So it can be with our losses, a muffled sadness which surfaces when we allow ourselves to be still. At night I close the double glazed windows to silence the sound of cars and, likewise, it is tempting for us to find ways to shut out or block the pain we have accumulated. We can use work, food, sex or substances to run from or dull the ache, but it will not resolve the underlying problem.

Talking to others on the subject it became clear that what I was feeling was far from unusual. It was the beginning of a search and gradual understanding which would lead me to set up workshops on dealing with loss and eventually to writing this book.

In the following pages we will share some personal stories and some ideas of how we can learn to neutralise our sense of loss whilst retaining a respect for, and an acknowledgement of, our experience.

To my mind, the most powerful opportunity for learning, growth and healing is to connect with others. How easy it is to imagine that what we have gone through in however many years we have been alive is unique. Yes we, as personalities, are all unique and so are our lives in their minutiae, but the human condition transcends our individuality, our separateness, and brings us into a state of common-ness.

I have based *The Loss Box* on this common-ness by talking to people of differing ages and asking them for their accounts on loss. Some have found a way of dealing with the wreckage of these various life events, large and small, but others have yet to do so.

For reasons of privacy I have used pseudonyms for the case

studies. Likewise, names within the main text have been changed. I am extremely grateful to each and every contributor for allowing us to have some insight into his or her life.

For many of us, the mere knowledge that others have suffered losses similarly, and that such happenings are an unavoidable part of being alive, might be sufficient to alleviate a sense of loss. For others, however, it is necessary to undergo a more intensive process. For this purpose I am including some exercises I use in my workshops and which I hope will be of help.

I trust you to "pick and mix". In other words, take what speaks to you, and discard what does not.

If you cannot bend the wind, bend the sails.

Chinese proverb

CHAPTER ONE

What is Loss?

We spend our lives forever taking leave.
Rilke

What is loss?

The obvious interpretation is loss of a loved one through death, but I am not intending to cover grief in this form. There are already numerous books on this painful subject.

I am not including trauma; happenings which may require expert help to resolve and which are beyond the scope of what we are dealing with here.

Rather, my interest is in the numerous losses or endings which inevitably occur in everyone's life but which often go unrecognised in their importance, and those that are more individual but which, nevertheless, do not qualify as a disaster or tragedy.

The term "loss" described in these pages embraces other words such as grief, regret, disappointment, disillusion, endings, goodbyes, parting, change and dissatisfaction. No doubt there are others.

So where do these losses go? For the purposes of this book I am suggesting we put them in our "loss box". This box tucks nicely into our solar plexus and doesn't bother us most of the time. In fact, in the early part of our lives we can be unaware of its existence.

Each time we have a loss we subconsciously open up the box to pop it in and then fasten the lid firmly down again. This suffices for a while but, hidden from view, the

1

unresolved grief quietly worries away at the contents and over the years things start to bubble and ferment.

Gradually the box fills up and on every reopening of the lid for a new loss, the existing, now rather rancid, losses try to escape. They want our attention. They want to be recognised. Their cumulative effect gives them a power beyond their individual weight.

When we are carrying around sadness in such a toxic state of fermentation, we suffer from what amounts to septicaemia of the soul. It is as though the underlying grief permeates our bloodstream.

In the following pages we will take an unflinching look at losses experienced from childhood onwards and the need to acknowledge them. Some losses will be more obviously distressing than others. Some may have a long-term impact whilst others do not. Some may appear inconsequential at the time of happening and might only be appreciated in their significance retrospectively.

There is no negativity in what we are attempting to do here. Quite the reverse; this is a book about facing reality with acceptance and compassion. It is about forgiveness of ourselves for wrong turns, forgiveness of others for past hurts, and forgiveness of life for not always doing as we bid. It is about being human.

★

I have lost the ability to laugh. It's not that I am a miserable person or a depressive but when I was young I would occasionally laugh so much I would have to clutch my stomach because it hurt. I remember sometimes rolling on the floor in an uncontrollable fit of laughter. That just doesn't happen anymore. I suppose I giggle now, but it's not quite the same thing as a good old belly laugh. I don't know if it's because of the sadnesses that have happened over the years, but something seems to have killed the eruptions of deep, deep laughter. Kate.

★

"Missing out syndrome" feeds our sense of loss. It is so easy to imagine that what would make us truly happy lies elsewhere; opportunities not presented or not taken. Later in life we may wrestle with the sense that we missed out somewhere along the line or be inclined to chastise ourselves for life choices we now perceive as lost possibilities. This is normal.

Patrick is an eminent professor working in a prestigious university. He has numerous books to his name and travels globally, giving talks on international relations. Despite his apparent achievements he sometimes questions whether he took the easy path by spending his working life in academia. He wonders how he would have fared in the challenging and cutthroat world of business, or if he could have made a more lasting contribution by means of another route. He speaks of a quiet nagging suspicion that he has missed out on a wider experience.

If you have had similar concerns, you are in good company.

For everybody, each decision or choice we make involves loss. The term "opportunity cost" is commonly used in economics to demonstrate what is lost in terms of alternatives when money is spent.

If we have £10,000 in our account and we decide to spend it on a replacement car, the opportunity cost is that it is no longer available for a trip round the world or the new kitchen we had our eye on.

Equally, if we follow one path we necessarily relinquish the other. If we decide to study medicine, we are unlikely to satisfy our interest in engineering. If we get married this year we may never fulfil our dream of backpacking solo around Africa.

Biddy's story is a case in point. Biddy had a steady boyfriend at home, but whilst working in Rome she fell deeply in love with an Italian. She was torn between staying in Italy or going home. Eventually she went back to the UK and married her longstanding boyfriend. They are still married forty years later with three grown-up children and several grandchildren. Like a lot of marriages, the path has not been smooth, however, and occasionally she wonders what might have happened if she had stayed in Rome. The chances are it would have been the same in reverse but, nevertheless, Biddy is conscious of a mild presiding sense of loss as a result of having had to make this difficult choice.

Gain can also be loss in any area – it is the opportunity cost of life and it is meant to be.

*

For those of us who are perfectionists, it is probable that we will suffer a greater sense of loss than most. The drive to meet the challengingly high standards we set in everything we do will almost inevitably lead to a disproportionate and self-inflicted feeling of failure at times. We need to adopt a more realistic mantra of "good enough" if we are not to cause ourselves unnecessary pain.

The same applies for those who like to control, as life is unlikely to dance to our tune. Certainly, the adage that life is what happens when you are waiting for something else is not without foundation. We have only a certain amount of influence over where life takes us.

Whatever our personal experiences of loss might be, and however minor each one may seem when considered individually, collectively the losses to which we are subject have the potential to result in a deep inner sadness as the years pass. That is, unless we deal with them.

The twentieth century thinker and philosopher, Krishnamurti, summed this up when he told his followers that it is not so much the experiences that cause the damage but the residue they leave behind. He refers to the mental and emotional scars, and the memories which pile up one on top of the other, causing sorrow. As we are unable to escape these experiences entirely, he writes that in order to prevent them "taking root in the soil of the mind", we learn to "die each day to every yesterday".

In writing *The Loss Box* I hope to reveal how we might achieve this end and to suggest ways that each of us may bear our losses as an integral part of our being without the accompanying grief. Most of all I want to heighten awareness of loss as a universal phenomenon, part of our shared humanity, and to encourage people to face it. Whilst there are losses which will be uncomfortable, there are also those which in retrospect, if we lighten up and allow them, will make us laugh.

Pioneering work in the 1980s linked writing about our feelings and improved health. It seems that a variety of common illnesses, both chronic and life threatening, can be relieved by written disclosure of painful memories, even if only to ourselves. I do not doubt that loss frequently features on the list of items needing to be processed.

There will be more on this "emotionally expressive writing" technique, the brainchild of American social psychologist Dr James Pennebaker, in one of the exercises contained in this book.

We will cover loss in a number of areas including hopes, dreams and aspirations, identity, role, confidence, power, authority, youth, relationships, energy, jobs, health, love, purpose, sexuality, independence, money and success. Put in a list like this, losses can seem overwhelmingly negative but the truth is that most of us who are lucky enough to live to old age will experience at least a number of these, if not all, at some stage, even if only temporarily.

It is true that endings can bring new life, provide space for new interests, new joys, new roads, but that does not negate the need to recognise and deal with the detritus of the endings themselves.

★

I grieve for that sense of wonder and awe we have as small children. When I am with my toddler grandson I can sometimes recapture it through his eyes. I see him pointing at an aeroplane making a trail in a blue sky or his excitement at a squirrel running up a tree, and it reminds me to be more observant and to notice what is going on around me. No doubt he will lose this constant joy in the little things of life too, as we all tend to do, but it is lovely whilst it lasts. Felicity.

★

This is not a book for victims. Victims tend to wallow in their condition and even thrive on it. This is a book for the vast majority of us, those who "get on with it". This stoical attitude is admirable in its way, but we also need to be aware that if loss is internalised without being processed it can become buried pain and unfinished business, which can cause us to become "stuck" emotionally, unable to move on and to grow.

In *The Language of Letting Go*, a book of daily readings, author Melody Beattie writes that most of us have said so many farewells that we resist change in any shape or form, not because it is bad, but in a vain attempt to avoid more loss.

★

When I was ten my father decided we should emigrate to Australia. I will never forget saying goodbye to my friends, and handing our family cat and my much loved guinea pig over to a neighbour to keep. I tried hard to be excited about this new life we were promised because I did not want to disappoint my parents, but the pain of leaving behind all that was familiar and precious is something that has never left me. Jack.

★

Not long after I passed my driving test in my late teens, I had a minor bump with another car on a roundabout. In my state of shock, my reaction was to continue driving, to put my foot down and keep going. I am not sure exactly what was going on in my head, but I know I wanted to distance myself from what had occurred and maybe even pretend it had not really happened. Quite understandably, the guy whose car I had knocked chased me and made me stop and go through the correct procedure.

This is exactly what so many of us do throughout our lives. When we suffer loss, instead of stopping and dealing with the emotional fall out, we put our foot to the floor and keep motoring. There comes a point, though, when life catches up with us and forces us to look at what has happened in our past.

Many of us will have seen clips on the news of people from other cultures wailing, throwing their hands in the air and letting their tears flow. Obviously our responses need to be in proportion to the loss experienced, but it seems to me that to a greater or lesser degree this is a healthy way to react to pain, to let it all out. For those of us who are born into a more emotionally restrained, or even repressed, society it is not how we are usually encouraged to behave. We are far more likely to push hurt down inside us, either to deny its existence or so we can process it privately in our own time.

Sometimes, as in my car bump, we feel a need to put a

distance between ourselves and the event in order to make sense of it. Once suppressed, however, the loss is often not dealt with despite our best intentions, because finding quiet time to process what happens in our lives is difficult. It is easier just to keep focusing on the road ahead, and to hold our foot hard down on the accelerator.

★

I lived in a university town where the neighbouring houses were occupied by students. This was no problem until a group of exceptionally rowdy young people moved in on one side. They played loud music until four or five each morning and after a year of trying to maintain a responsible job on very little sleep I reached a point of nervous collapse and moved out. Part of my recovery included seeing a counsellor who pointed out to me that what I was suffering from was loss. I had lost the security of knowing my home was a safe place, a sanctuary to which I could return at the end of the day. The extraordinary thing was that once we addressed the idea of loss, lots of other losses came up from the past too as if I had opened the floodgates. My therapist uncovered so many tears. Petra.

★

Our losses may be great or they may be small, but believe me when I tell you they are there. It is true for me, for you, for the person sitting beside you on the bus or the train, for the man or woman in front of you in the supermarket queue. Some people may live in denial, but that does not mean they are immune; they have just shut down as a survival technique.

In my case there were a small number of substantial losses surrounded by a myriad of less demanding ones, but put them all together and my loss box was bulging at the seams. The premise of this book is that it doesn't have to be like that; we can change this less than desirable state of affairs.

★

When I started writing this book I visualised my loss box as brown with metal strips up the sides, like a miniature pirate treasure chest. Now that I have decided to befriend my loss box and the losses I have squirreled away over the years, I have changed it to something more cheerful. I have mentally covered it in a bright yellow patterned fabric, like a Breton table cloth.

Participants in my workshops have come up with other interesting interpretations. One saw it as a fine gold silk drawstring bag and another as a large green crocodile skin purse with a very strong zip. It doesn't matter how we picture it as long as it works for us, but in the following chapters I will continue to refer to the loss box.

Facing ourselves requires courage and if you feel a need for professional support then find someone with whom you are comfortable and in whom you have every confidence.

If you are more at ease working through your losses by yourself, with a friend or in a group, you will find a few suggestions of how this might be approached included in the book. In the end, however, we all have to discover our own way of dealing with loss and grief. The important thing is that we do it.

Our losses are part of who we are, of our history, but the hurt that surrounds them does not have to be carried forward into our future.

★

I look back on my youth and realise how much I missed out through fear and lack of confidence. I never ventured out of my comfort zone. Now that I have acquired more self-esteem with age I see how much more I could have done and achieved. I lost out on so much. Vanessa.

My loss box is nowhere near empty yet, and I still experience occasional times of sorrow over what is missing in my life, what I hoped would happen but which has not, what has happened which I would rather had not, the failures, goodbyes and the endings, but I am getting there at my own pace.

The difference is I am now able to identify the source of the sadness and rationalise my thought processes before they take me down too dark a tunnel. It leaves me free to celebrate all that is good, and there is so much more that is good. I am able to balance loss with resulting gain and to know that, in the end, this is just part of being fully alive.

Inevitably, there will be losses in the future too, but I hope that with my new knowledge I will be wise enough to deal with them as they occur and my loss box will eventually be redundant. I hope the same for you too.

Everything we really accept undergoes a change.
Katherine Mansfield

CHAPTER TWO

Childhood

The way is to begin with the beginning.
Lord Byron

I am a loser. You are a loser. The general wear and tear of life means every one of us is a loser. We have all had numerous losses to contend with and overcome, and in this book we will hopefully learn to acknowledge and celebrate our survival.

When do these losses first appear? I believe it is early in childhood, and as we do not have the where-with-all to understand what is going on, or to process the hurt, these are the first to be deposited in the loss box.

It has been suggested that the initial loss we meet is birth itself. I can see that having been tucked up in a warm, cosy, protected environment, it must be bordering on traumatic to be thrust into the world.

It is no wonder that when we suffer mental, emotional, or physical pain we often curl up into the embryonic position, as if we are back in the womb. According to a cranio-sacral therapist I interviewed, it is common for her clients to revert to this physical position as she releases their emotional blockages during treatment sessions.

Could the subconscious loss of being enclosed safely inside our mother's body explain why so many of us feel such a primal and intense need to be part of a couple, as if to re-conjoin, and why the prospect of being alone can hold so much irrational fear?

It is through love relationships that we try to transcend our separation, our aloneness, and recapture wholeness. It may also be that in addition to the sensual and erotic pleasure during sex there is comfort in two bodies becoming one again, however fleetingly.

There is considerable research being carried out on the emotional and psychological after-effects of birth for the infant, some symptoms of which might prove to stay with us throughout life.

The possible lasting impact of the birth experience on a newborn has been recognised since the early twentieth century when Otto Rank, an associate of Sigmund Freud, developed a specific form of psychoanalysis to deal with this area of interest. The subject matter went out of fashion for a number of years but is now regaining interest. Rank's book *The Trauma of Birth* is still available today.

My children were born in the sixties and seventies. At that time it was standard practice for mothers to hold their babies only for a few minutes after birth, before they were whisked away to another room and stuck in a cot amongst hoards of other possibly wailing infants. It was also normal to stay in hospital for a week or more, during which time the babies were brought to the mother's bed at four hourly intervals to be fed, and parents were not encouraged in the nursery.

The abrupt loss of constant human contact and connection must have been a shock for those dear little new arrivals. I appreciated the rest and the recovery time I was allowed, but in retrospect I think it may be the case that both my babies and I lost something much more valuable.

★

When a new infant appears in the family, existing children can lose their status. Perhaps we were the only child and now we

12

have to watch our parents give their attention to this crying bundle whose demands appear to exceed ours.

Alternatively, we are one of a number of children but our position is nevertheless usurped by an interloper and the dynamics of our life as we have known it have changed to accommodate a stranger. We want to love this little one, but part of us is also wounded by the loss of how it used to be. Our parents' attention has to be spread further, and our share is necessarily reduced.

Esme's story highlighted this potential for loss when she told me she had never completely recovered from the arrival of her brother when she was two years old. Coming in from the garden, she had inadvertently allowed the kitchen door to bang as it closed. Her mother, who was at the sink, turned sharply and scolded her, telling her that her baby brother was asleep and that she must not make any noise. At that moment, she recalls, it was like another door had closed inside her, and that she had been shut out. From that time onwards, she felt less important than her younger sibling.

Esme is in her early sixties now, but her sense of being second best has not diminished with the years. This is not to lay unnecessary blame on Esme's mother who, no doubt, had little or no concept of the unintended damage she had done with this reactive remark, possibly under stress. This is life.

There is a degree of alchemy here. I know from the differing reactions my sister and I had to our upbringing, that the exact same situation can create varying results according to the mixture of the personalities involved. What can cause a certain reaction in one child, and perhaps a lasting one as in the case of Esme, can affect another differently or not at all.

George so resented the arrival of his baby brother, Max, that he metamorphosed overnight into a child his parents could scarcely recognise.

For nearly a year he became frequently aggressive,

belligerent, obstructive and deliberately defiant. On several occasions he asked if this "thing" could be sent back because he did not want a baby in the house. His poor mother and father were exhausted with dealing with such a changed personality.

When, after eighteen months of this untenable situation, the boys were made to share a bedroom, everything changed; the two became a team and the storm abated. The darling, funny, loving boy his parents had previously known suddenly reappeared as if he had been on a trip somewhere, and had slipped back unseen off the midnight train.

This little fellow had obviously been deeply affected by losing his place in the family set-up, and no matter how hard his mother and father had worked to reassure him and make him feel valued, his hurt, fury and frustration had been coming out sideways.

Nowadays, despite the inevitable sibling scraps and rivalries, George talks proudly of his little brother. Nevertheless, I have no doubt this has gone into his personal loss box.

In *Cider with Rosie*, Laurie Lee writes poignantly of his disbelief and utter dismay when, at the age of three, he lost his place in his mother's bed to his baby brother Tony. Up to that moment he had felt special amongst his siblings; he was the one who was privileged, who had a secret nightlife cuddling up to his mother's sleeping form. He had believed he was "her chosen companion, chosen from all for her extra love". What a loss that must have been for him.

There are those, conversely, who have grown up without siblings, but who would consider this a loss too. Whilst a single child has the undivided attention of its parents, it also shoulders their hopes and expectations and is deprived of young companionship in the home. He or she must learn to play alone and become self-sufficient. For some this might prove not to be a problem, they may even thrive on it, but others may suffer from isolation or be overwhelmed by the concentrated parental focus.

It would seem that whatever the make-up of our family, it is likely we will experience loss in one way or another. This is the way of the world.

★

On Christmas Eve my sister and I crept into the guest bedroom where our grandmother was staying, to see if we could find where she had hidden our Christmas presents. We discovered a bag of small, unwrapped presents under the bed which we supposed must be from her. Early the next morning we opened our stockings to find those exact items from Father Christmas. Obviously we could not admit we had seen them before, but I remember the feeling of loss when I realised Father Christmas did not exist. I also lost my belief that parents always tell the truth. Geraldine.

★

As I write of early childhood I am immediately taken back to my introductory day at nursery school. I must have been three or four years old. I can see the building clearly in my mind, and I remember looking around and wondering if everyone else felt as scared as I did. For the first time in my life I was conscious of being without the cloak of protection my mother's presence provided. I did not doubt she would come back to collect me, but I was no longer confident the world was a safe place. Life was never quite the same again.

This is just a minor example of early loss, but the fact that merely by reflecting on childhood I was immediately transported back to that occasion, and could feel the anxiety again, means the experience has stayed with me in some capacity.

Asked how school was going, five-year-old Hal told his aunt that he was in love with Emma, who was in his class, but that she was not in love with him. Another classmate, Hattie, on the other hand, was in love with him, but he was not in love with her. This news was delivered with great seriousness, but minutes later Hal was distracted by dressing up as a super hero and concentrated on saving the world in his living room. Nevertheless, this is an example of how, in childhood, we prepare for the adult life to come. More complex relationship issues at a later age will no doubt require more than a Spider Man or Batman outfit to sort them out.

Not all loss of innocence is so benign, however. Emily and her young son, Theo, were on an outing when they were the victims of road rage. When they came to a halt in a queue at a city road junction, a stranger started attacking their car. He was hitting and kicking the vehicle, screaming abuse and trying to smash through the window beside where the child was sitting. Luckily the police arrived quickly and the man, who was drunk, was arrested and taken away.

In this moment Theo learned that the world is not made up entirely of people who have his best interests at heart. Consequently, when his grandmother set out on a journey not long afterwards, he was full of concern for her safety.

A small child's grazed knee from a fall can be kissed better by a loving parent, and if someone snatches our toy there is usually an adult to sort it out on our behalf. As we grow, however, we have to let go of the idea that outsiders can cure all our ills, and we need to learn self-reliance. Once we go to school we are largely expected to cope with day-to-day problems and upsets and, to a large degree, lose our dependence on another.

★

When I was sent to boarding school at eight years old, my source of comfort was "Kanga", an old, worn and much loved toy kangaroo. I used to press his tail under my nose inhaling deeply until I drifted into sleep. Kanga followed me to my senior school where one night I came up to my dormitory to find he was gone. A frantic search took place helped by the other girls, but to no avail. In tears I went to ask the help of Matron who told me grimly that Kanga was disgusting, and she had thrown him away. I suppose she was trying to get me to grow up, but I wasn't ready. She will never know the effect that loss had on me. Claire.

★

All change, even positive change, requires adjustment. Whilst venturing into new territory is stimulating, parting from what we are acquainted with and what we deem safe also involves a degree of loss, a leaving behind of the old and loss of the known.

Moving from one level of schooling to the next can come into this category. It is likely that we have been gaining confidence as we progressed through junior school to the top class. For the final year we have been one of the "big" boys or girls. However exciting it is to move to the senior school, it requires us to start right down at the bottom again. We lose the position of superiority we held at our junior school, and we lose the familiarity of where to hang our school bag, or the location of the classroom, the gym or the dining room. We may have left behind a class teacher in whom we put our trust, and the support system of our friends and classmates if they do not come with us.

Obviously we overcome these hurdles with time, but such changes represent losses which may need careful handling.

Later, this process is repeated if we go to university, or when we are the new man or woman in the workplace, although hopefully we will deal with these altered circumstances with less disruption as we mature.

The concept of a job for life is no longer the norm and it is commonplace for people to move geographically when they transfer to a new employer to pursue their careers. This uprooting of the family, this triple whammy of leaving a house, school, and friendships, can be a source of great loss to a child.

My parents loved doing up houses and moving just for the sake of it, something I have inherited, and as a result I changed schools and localities a number of times in childhood. One result of this mildly peripatetic lifestyle was that I failed to learn how to make lasting friendships in my young life. Possibly as a result, such friendships have become a priority in adulthood, and I have been consciously determined to make up for this loss.

★

With the current high divorce rate, the potential for grief in the lives of children is obvious. As someone who has subjected my children to this experience, I know that however civilised we try to be in dealing with a family break-up, the children suffer loss.

Any of us would be fooling ourselves if we indulged in the confident belief that our relationship decisions did not impact on our offspring. How can it be otherwise? When a marriage ends, one parent leaves the home and the family is no longer complete. If one or both parents remarry, often with the introduction of stepfamilies as rivals for affection, the children may feel confused or displaced.

If, on the other hand, there is no parting but there is serious discord within the home, the child has to let go of its instinctive need for a happy and harmonious environment.

No matter how the adults may attempt to cover up their relationship difficulties, children have an uncanny knack of picking up on undercurrents, even if this remains at a subconscious level.

Family is the school of love, it is where we learn how relationships work or, conversely, do not work. A child who grows up with parents who show love, respect and concern for each other, is taught a vital lesson in loving. Those who do not have such parents are deprived of this teaching and lose out.

I will not delve in detail into the complex area of marital unhappiness or break-up and its effect because this borders on trauma, and that is not the subject we are addressing. It is, however, such a prevalent experience for young people that it seems important to include it, even if only in passing.

★

More than one friend of mine has experienced loss in childhood through the disability or long-term illness, mental or physical, of a sibling. In these cases the attention of the parents was almost entirely directed to the sick brother or sister and the remaining child or children were more or less left to cope on their own. Such youngsters were forced to grow up before their time and lost out on much of their childhood.

The same is true when a parent is an invalid, or mentally or physically ill, where the young members of the family take on a premature responsibility for the running of the household or for their own self care emotionally or practically. There may be a reversal of roles where, by necessity, the young person becomes the carer for the parent. In such instances, the freedom to be a child is largely non-existent.

★

My mother had a breakdown when I was a baby and she was in hospital during a crucial period in which children form attachments. Whilst this was going on I stayed with my grandparents, aunt and cousin where life was fun, there was laughter, and I felt safe. My cousin was a little older than me and he became my surrogate brother. When my mother recovered her health sufficiently to cope I was taken back to live with my parents. I remained an only child and my days were spent treading on eggshells in fear of my mother's instability, panic attacks and tantrums. I longed for those times when I could be with my extended family again, and especially my cousin, but when I was seven my aunt and cousin went to live in America. The sadness of firstly losing the security, fun, freedom and the permission to be a child which I had experienced whilst staying with my grandparents, and then losing my aunt and my cousin have remained with me into adulthood. Mandy.

★

From talking to younger generations I am hopeful that the attitude to boys and crying is changing from how it was when I was growing up. I did not have brothers so am not in a position to quote first-hand of this stiff upper lip, character building philosophy being imposed in childhood, but some men have told me that tears were unacceptable in their youth, and that as a result they find themselves unable to weep even at times when it might be appropriate or expected.

Being a constant "blubberer" is unacceptable in adulthood regardless of whether it is a man or woman, but as occasional crying is nature's outlet for extreme pain, sadness and grief, loss of this healthy and cathartic form of expression based on gender does not seem to make sense.

In his autobiography, *Losing my Virginity*, Richard Branson describes how he threw up in his bed on his first night at boarding school. He was not quite eight years old and he was

20

vomiting not because of illness, but through anxiety. He has spoken of feeling the humiliation as the matron made him clean the sheets. It is hard to imagine how any child undergoing such an experience could fail to lose a degree of trust in the kindness of adults. If our mother and father are there to care for us, protect and defend us, how can it be that they volunteer us for such a happening? If the matron's job is to look after our welfare, what impact would such misplaced discipline have on a young, impressionable mind?

Also aged eight, Jonny was sent to preparatory school quite a distance from where he lived. He came home for school holidays and half terms but there were no weekend outings, parental visits or telephone calls allowed. Each week he wrote a compulsory letter to his mother and father which was censored, so he could not tell them of his unhappiness. His parents joked that the letters were hard to read because his tears had smudged the ink, yet they did not seem to register his obvious distress.

It is difficult to discuss this with him because he finds it almost impossible to talk about his feelings, but I believe he shut down emotionally at this time. Now in late middle age, Jonny has never married, allows few close friendships, and fears intimacy of any kind. I suspect he lost his faith in loving relationships when he was that vulnerable little boy.

From my personal knowledge of similarly aged men from the same class background and history, this scenario is not unusual. I am aware that some personalities have thrived under similar circumstances, and I would not wish to generalise, but whilst Jonny's reaction of eschewing any relationships whatsoever may be extreme, many I know demonstrate difficulty in relating to others in any depth and to showing emotion.

The accepted thinking at that time was that sending a young boy away, even at such a tender age, would make "a man" of him, but what I see of much of this middle-class male generation is that it has stunted their emotional development.

By removing boys from the nurture of the home environment before they were ready, and placing them in unsympathetic, "toughening up" all male conditions, it may be they lost something precious.

The story does not end there, though, because as adults these men would enter relationships and marriages without the ability to connect at an emotional level, so their wives and partners, and possibly their children, also had to deal with the consequences of this loss.

★

I have been married for a long time to a man who is unable to show affection. It is hard to know if I still love him or whether it is just habit. I suppose he loves me, but he does not tell me he does, and he does not show it physically either, other than in bed where it is a sexual act rather than loving. I am a very tactile person so this has been hard to bear. I have stayed in the marriage for the sake of our children, but now they have left I think it is too late to start again by myself. It is so sad because he is such a good man really and he is kind; he just cannot deal with emotion. The word loss scarcely covers it. Val.

★

In 1990 the psychotherapist and author, Nick Duffell, founded Boarding School Survivors. BSS offers workshops and courses to those who, like himself, feel they have paid a high price for their boarding school education and need to process what they have experienced.

Although many young girls of my vintage were also sent away to school, they do not appear to have suffered the same fate, or perhaps not to the same degree. Mostly they were sent when they were older, and emotional expression seems to have been encouraged, or at least tolerated.

Ginny's story differs in that she was sent to school on the opposite side of the world. Ginny's father was based in Hong Kong for most of his working life. In the mid 1950s, at the age of twelve, Ginny was sent to an all girls' school deep in the English countryside where she knew no one. Apart from the landline telephone, technology to keep in touch over long distances did not exist then and she had to rely on weekly letters. She went home to see her parents once every year in the summer, but because of the absence of contact they had become more or less strangers to her. The remaining two annual holidays were spent at a special home with about thirty other children. Ginny believes that if the woman who ran the home had been a warm, motherly type it might have been easier, but she was a harridan and Ginny found her a strict and frightening figure.

The loss of family life in childhood and adolescence is a deeply buried pain for Ginny, the awareness of which has emerged as she has got older. She has always known what she missed out on, but only with age has she reached a full realisation of the toll it has taken.

Luckily technology, improved long distance travel and the changing attitudes of society and employment make this a tale of woe which is much less likely to be repeated in today's world.

Boarding schools have changed almost unrecognisably in recent years, the pupils have increased contact with home through the term time, many establishments are mixed sex, and there is more awareness around the pitfalls I have mentioned.

When one of my grandchildren starting boarding recently, he was linked to an established pupil whose responsibility it was to help with the settling in period. This was excellent for both parties, and the two became firm friends. Hopefully, with these more humane practices in place, such losses to which I have previously referred will be minimised.

★

I can easily transport myself back into a teenage party scenario in the early 1960s, where all the boys were at one end of the room and the girls at the other. By being separated in single sex schools throughout our education we had lost the opportunity to develop an easy relationship with each other. Daring to cross the intervening space wasn't so much a matter of "mind the gap" as "leap the chasm".

★

School life involves learning to deal with loss irrespective of whether we are sent away to board or not, and whether we are educated privately or by the state.

Our friend decided he or she preferred someone else to spend time with during the playground break. We were not invited to join the gang we so admired. We were not picked for the orchestra, the school play or we were dropped from the football team. We developed spots. We did not get the prize for maths as we had secretly hoped, or we lost our position as top of the class in English. The redhead on whom we had a crush did not return our admiring glances or deserted us for the guy who played the guitar.

We may look back on these happenings and wonder what the fuss was all about, but at the time such matters were deadly serious and destined for the loss box.

Hopefully these losses are outweighed by the more positive outcomes, of which there are no doubt many, but nevertheless it is a preparation for life.

★

I had a baby when I was a teenager. This was in the early sixties, when such things were hushed up. My son was a product of a relationship which was not destined to end in marriage so my parents organised for the baby to be adopted and I went along with the arrangements because I didn't know what else I could do. I will not go into detail about this part of the story because it qualifies as personal trauma. However, about five years ago my son, Will, and I met. I made some enquiries about him and it turned out he was looking for me too. It has not always been easy getting to know each other, and there have been issues to deal with, but we are both determined to keep working at it. We have supper together every week and each time we learn a little more about each other. I am acutely aware, however, of the huge void that is his past and in which I had no part. Nothing can really bring that back. We are both victims of the social mores of the time, and although I am hopeful we will share our lives from now on, I am also very much aware that we have lost nearly forty years of loving and being together. Charlotte.

★

When we are very young most of us believe our parents have all the answers; they are the source of all knowledge. How unsettling it is as we grow older to realise that this is not the case, that we are not clutched to the bosom of universal wisdom; our parents are just regular people who know some stuff but don't know other stuff.

This is a loss that slips in almost unnoticed by most and is often followed by a period when we think our parents don't know anything at all. Our mothers and fathers have never been young; they have never "lived", had sex, known passion, or done anything remotely adventurous or exciting. They cannot be trusted to understand.

This is the time when we have to start venturing out into the world as ourselves rather than extensions of those who love us; we have to break away, "lose" our dependence. For some this naissance of individuality may be plain sailing, a release, whereas for others it is a time of uncertainty, loneliness and overwhelming angst.

★

I have a need to look at when and with whom I lost my virginity. I was only in my early teens and I was not emotionally mature enough to really understand what I was giving away. My parents had not talked to me about sex so in a pre-internet era most of what I knew came from older girls who had been experimenting and were showing off their knowledge by telling us what was what. I think I was too scared to say no, so I not only lost the irretrievable state of virginity, I lost the chance to make it something special. That is a real regret. Jilly.

★

Leaving the protection that parental love and care has provided for us up to now is a life passage during which we can feel supremely confident one minute, and unbearably vulnerable the next. It is a time of immense excitement, boundless opportunity, challenge and fear.

Children growing up and becoming independent is summed up in the last two lines of Cecil Day Lewis's poem *Walking Away*. "… selfhood begins with a walking away, And love is proved in the letting go". There is loss for both parties.

Watching my eldest grandchild approach his teens, I am aware he has temporarily lost his place in the social set-up. At fourteen he is no longer a child in many ways, although when he is with his younger cousin he can slip back into playing games of imagination quite happily.

Despite the slight swagger and the ultra cool haircut, he is not yet eligible for the status of fully fledged teenager either, and I can feel his sense of being lost when I am with him. I wish I could help, but I know he needs to find his own tentative way within the supportive framework his family and his circle of friends provide.

★

There is no "pointing the bony finger" involved in the approach to awareness contained here, but more of an appreciation that it is not possible to grow up without having losses. These painful episodes teach us to stand on our own two feet and help us to become individuals, and all of us react differently to these happenings according to our personalities and upbringing.

Most of the losses to which I refer are neither good nor bad; they just are. It is how we deal with them that dictates how they impact on our futures.

All changes, even the most longed for, have their melancholy; for what we leave behind us is a part of ourselves; we must die to one life before we can enter another.

Anatole France

EXERCISE 1

In Chapter One I referred to the scientific research inspired by James Pennebaker, which involves translating emotional upheavals by putting them down on paper. In so doing we can create a story which helps us understand what went on for us; something it is evidently more difficult to do through the spoken word, even in therapy, or whilst it remains "in our head".

This is referred to as "labelling", and in the years since Dr Pennebaker's breakthrough work in this field, numerous studies have shown a positive connection not only between writing therapy and improved physical health but, more recently, with cognitive ability and memory also.

Roughly, the Pennebaker method is to write for around fifteen minutes per day for three to four days; it is not advised to go beyond this timescale. *"Emotionally expressive writing"* should be written for ourselves so it can be entirely candid although, if we so wish, we can share it with another once it is completed. Either way, it has proved to be a healing process for those larger and more damaging hurts we are holding within.

Alternatively, writing a letter to ourselves is a common tool used by counsellors. This is a variation of the above I would offer here as an exercise to make sense of our less dramatic childhood losses.

We can write one letter or many and there is no restriction on time. I would suggest only one rule; each letter must be compassionate.

For those less difficult losses we can make our correspondence amusing as we recall the ridiculous hairdo we affected as we tried and failed to attract that boy in Year 5. We can gently forgive ourselves for when we pretended to be something we were not just to impress and instead ended up looking like a complete loser.

We can write healing words to the child, who is us, who was scared of the bullying teacher, and through whom we lost confidence in ourselves.

We can console ourselves when we remember the humiliation of having no one to partner for the two-legged race on sports day.

So what if we hated football or netball, that sport was not one of our strengths and no one wanted us on their team. We can remind ourselves of those things we could do well, even if it was climbing trees or making chocolate biscuit cake.

We can comfort that small person who still resides in us and who passed his/her exams with flying colours after a great deal of effort, but who still failed to get the attention or admiration of his/her parents.

What could we write to the adolescent who looked in the mirror and saw someone who was not good enough?

How could we make reparation for those years lost when we had acne or put on puppy fat and were too self-conscious of our appearance to approach the opposite sex?

Whether we post the letter back to our adult selves to keep or whether we burn it or float it down a river or stream (see a later exercise for more on this) is up to us and what we consider would be the most effective action.

What we decide to do with the letter once it is written is less important than how we sign it. I suggest the words "With great love".

CHAPTER THREE

This is Not How I Saw it!

The unexamined life is not worth living.
Socrates

For most thinking people there comes a time when reflection creeps in, invited or not. This "taking stock" can happen at any stage but, from my observation, is most commonly experienced in our thirties and forties. It may be triggered by a traumatic event such as losing a job, the death or illness of a loved one or some other happening which shakes us out of our chrysalis, our enclosed world. Equally it can come upon us stealthily, gradually unsettling our equilibrium.

We can try to ignore it for a while but eventually, if we are lucky, it will take a megaphone straight to our ear and demand that we listen to what is going on inside us.

I say "if we are lucky" because although more extreme examples of this emotional turmoil are known as a midlife crisis or even a breakdown, I would prefer to call the milder version a midlife gift or friend.

Reflection is not necessarily comfortable, but that can be its purpose. We are being given an awakener, an opportunity to implement changes that need to be made and to refresh and renew our lives in whatever way is appropriate to us.

Of all the losses in our lives, loss of "how we thought it would be" is probably the most insidious. Whether you prefer to call it disappointment or regret rather than loss is up to you, but this area of potential sadness is of the utmost importance. We need to deal with it if we are not to grow into bitter old people, and what could be worse than being a cantankerous, frustrated, unfulfilled person at the end of our lives? Let us avoid the "grumpy old git" syndrome at all costs.

Loss of the way we saw things turning out is a common reality, a component of the human condition and an ingredient of life it is virtually impossible to sidestep. The reason it becomes a problem is that we do not tend to talk about it openly, and very rarely to those closest to us in case it appears to reflect badly on them or perhaps on the relationship.

When I first heard of the Buddhist teaching of detachment I misconstrued its meaning and thought it involved not caring deeply about people or things in general, keeping emotionally distant and aloof, a sentiment I found hard to accept. Now I have learned its true interpretation I believe it is a wisdom we ignore at our peril.

For those who do not know about detachment, it is a way of "letting go" and "letting be". If we want a particular outcome in any area of our lives, the teaching tells us to do everything reasonable to make it happen and then allow ourselves to remain in a state of active non-attachment. To play with the words of Rudyard Kipling, we need to dream but not make dreams our master.

If our aspirations come to fruition, that is good, but if they do not, that is acceptable too. If we are determined to stay "attached", if we hang on with white knuckles to things being as we envisaged, we cause ourselves unnecessary levels of pain. We are inviting loss.

It is a fundamental truth that just because we want something, even with all our heart, it does not automatically follow that it is right for us. One of the oft repeated mantras of parenting I remember most is that we do not always get what we want. When I went further and told my children that, instead, perhaps we get what we need, I could sense their exasperation, which I sympathise with even now. I do believe, however, it is true more often than it is not and that our hopes, dreams and intentions may clash with our destiny. That is the way life is.

★

In any discussion which includes having a set plan for how things will turn out, I am reminded of the film *Sliding Doors* which shows two scenarios.

In the early part of the story the heroine runs down steps to catch a train and in one version she is held up momentarily by a child across her path so that the doors to the train close as she reaches the platform. The alternative version is that she is not obstructed on the stairs and just manages to board the train before it pulls out.

The consequences of these two outcomes are then played out side by side, showing the differing courses her life takes as a result. The essence of the film is that this small incident, a split-second delay, has the power to direct her future.

If it is that easy for our lives to change direction, how can we seriously expect our plans to play out precisely as we foresaw in our youth?

★

Humans appear to have an inbuilt psychological need for certainty, even though the only true certainty is that there is no such thing. Seeking certainty causes untold misery and loss if not held in check.

One of the themes which recur frequently in self-help books is that everything happens "perfectly". This sentiment does not work for me. Perhaps I am crabby, but it seems to me that very little in life is perfect. I am happier saying "It's alright". If we are achieving or have achieved our dreams and aspirations more or less, that is great. If not, unless we have been subject to a tragedy, that is alright too.

Where we are, who we are, what we have are alright (and if it truly is not, then do something to change your situation where possible because life is too precious to spend being unhappy). Merely because it is not as we had thought it would be does not automatically mean it is wrong or second best. It just is.

★

How many deskbound office workers originally dreamed of being pilots, actors, athletes, pop stars or artists?

A psychotherapist once told me one of the most common areas of distress for his clients was that they have not found it possible to earn a living doing what made their heart sing. The dichotomy of bringing in a reliable and sufficient wage in order to survive in practical terms, but also longing to pursue an interest which fulfils our purpose emotionally and spiritually, is a common one it seems.

The fortunate few are able to build a career on what they love doing, but for vast numbers this is not the case. Where possible, those interests not satisfied in our work can still play a role in the form of a hobby.

Natalie works for the local authority in an administrative capacity which provides her with security but little in the way of expression. When she comes home, however, she has a choice. Will she go up to the spare bedroom where she is writing a novel? Or will she go into the kitchen, one corner of which contains her easel, so she can work at her abstract painting?

Few people who employ Bill to decorate their homes will be aware that he dedicates his spare time to writing plays. He has the agreement of his wife and children that he can spend two evenings a week in his insulated shed at the bottom of the garden doing what he finds most fulfilling. They know they will benefit too because getting this out of his system makes him a happier person to be around. Several of his creations have been performed locally but he has not had a big break yet. Undeterred, he continues with his passion.

Similarly, each Wednesday evening, estate agent Carol heads off to rehearse with a choir. Carol, who lives with her elderly blind mother, has a superb soprano voice and considered singing professionally in her youth. Instead she opted for what she decided was a more secure career. Her choir is of a very high standard and travels nationwide to perform. Carol enjoys her work and is more than happy to care for her mother with whom she has a good relationship, but it is when she is singing that she truly feels alive.

If we are lucky enough to have an interest or passion, and most of us have if we search for it, we need to express it or we will suffer loss.

★

My chosen career was set design, but at the time I was applying for a college place there were only two options of where to study. The standard was so high that for the first college only eight applicants out of over a hundred were accepted and I was not one of them. I was also turned down by the second. I thought theatrical costume might offer me a route into theatre design as I had A-level needlework, as well as Art and English, but that also turned out to be a dead end. I have worked in many different fields subsequently, including design, and have allowed life to take me down an assortment of roads in terms of my career, but occasionally I still feel wistful that I never fulfilled my dream of working in the theatre. Izzy.

★

In *The Empty Raincoat,* Charles Handy, author, philosopher, management guru and co-founder of the London Business School, writes of those who dedicate their lives to climbing the career ladder only to find when they get to the top rung that it has been leaning against the wrong wall.

The inference here is that loss can also result from achievement of our plans and dreams where these have proved to be misguided or inappropriate to who we are. We can become so fixated on achieving a goal set in our youth, that we miss the fact that we have changed in the interim and that this specific objective no longer holds meaning for us.

Can we be sure that if our lives had gone according to the plan of our imagination, that if we had become chairman of a multi-national, sailed solo around the globe, made a fortune on the stock exchange, won Wimbledon, an Oscar or the Turner Prize, topped the music charts, dropped out and become a traveller, or earned a living as a diving instructor in the Seychelles, we would be any happier than we are now? Of course, it is possible that we could be, but it is not a given.

The distorted values of our consumer society make it easy for the average man or woman to believe that if he/she could swap his/her humble abode for a grand house with grounds and a swimming pool, the family's battered people carrier (probably full of half-eaten packets of crisps and discarded toffee papers) for a gleaming Porsche, his/her aspirations would be realised. Material possessions, however, do not provide immunity from loss. To reach such a pinnacle, other dreams may have to be sacrificed on the way. Having it all is rarely more than an illusion.

★

How many of us have a niggling feeling that our ambitions have been curtailed through fear? Fear of failure, fear of success, fear of stepping out of our comfort zone, fear of making a fool of ourselves are very real stumbling blocks to fulfilling our hopes and dreams.

If we allow ourselves to believe we are alone in experiencing these anxieties, we only need to open ourselves up to others to discover how common this predicament is in people from all walks of life. Even those who have learned to break through these limiting instincts, and have achieved high-flying goals, may need to fight an ongoing battle with fear.

If we are not able to overcome our fears, despite our best efforts, it may be we are more suited to setting our sights realistically for our personality. If this is the case, we need to be careful not to put our decision to stay comparatively safe into our loss box. We have done what is right for us, and perhaps what we gain in our greater serenity outweighs the stress of testing ourselves beyond what is psychologically beneficial for who we are.

It is healthy to go to the edge, but whereas it is right for some to make a calculated leap and for others to close their eyes and jump, it is wiser for many to step back. If we have had the courage to go to the edge and look over, we will have gained a broader perspective and that may be all we need. We can then decide which outcome is best for us without incurring loss. It is those who do not undertake that initial exploration, those who are too frightened even to acknowledge that the wider view exists, that risk losing out as a result of fear.

★

I reached out for the telephone on my desk at work but suddenly became paralysed with anxiety. I was working in public relations and I was about to phone a contact on one of the national newspapers. I could not key in the number, and my brain froze. I left work early and went to the doctor who diagnosed extreme stress. As in many lines of work such as sales, those in public relations have to be able to deal with rejection. As it happens, rejection is something I have always found difficult to handle. I had some counselling after this incident and came to terms with the fact that I was in the wrong line of business. I had pushed and pushed myself to overcome fears and to achieve, and I had done well, but the cost to my mental, emotional and physical health was too high. I decided to change my career path and found something more suitable for my personality. I have never regretted it and will not be putting that in my loss box. Di.

★

The dreams and aspirations of youth are essential to motivate us but they are only that – dreams and aspirations. Some people achieve what they set out to, but many do not. This is no reason to negate what each one of us has done. If we do not recognise those dreams for what they are, just dreams and thought processes, we can miss what we have in the present and we can fail to appreciate that our lives may have been equally fulfilled in alternative ways.

Not all of us, however, had burning ambitions or achievements in mind as we approached adulthood. Instead, there may have been a subconscious sense of how things would turn out without too much effort on our part.

Regardless of whether we had set goals or a vague sense of direction, the future can be determined by unforeseen events and take us on a journey we never envisaged.

Mary's story is an example of how our lives can take an unexpected turn. Mary would never have foreseen spending the last thirty years firstly as a single mother of three children, and subsequently living alone.

As someone whose central ambition was to be the perfect

homemaker with a happy marriage and family life, and who believed strongly in love and commitment, she had not imagined getting divorced.

The loss of her intention to provide a stable, two parent upbringing for her children has been painful, but it has strengthened her commitment to being a supportive mother even further, and her closeness with her adult children has endured through times of crisis, theirs and hers.

Living without a loving partnership has been an enormous grief to Mary but she is aware that the aloneness she has so reluctantly borne has been the grit in the oyster which has irritated her into doing much more with her life than she might otherwise have done. If marriage had brought her the contentment she was seeking, as she imagined it would, it is possible she could have lost out on so much that has brought her satisfaction from other sources.

This is not to imply that such acceptance is easy, or that it does not require regularly renewed determination. What Mary's attitude does stress, however, is that going beyond "how we thought it would be" is possible.

★

I have two grown-up daughters, both of whom are gay. They and their respective partners are in their forties now so they are just past the age when they could take advantage of the new acceptance of both sex families, where children are born using donor sperm. As a result I will never have grandchildren. Initially I found this difficult to accept, and when I saw people my age with young children the hurt I felt was a physical pain. I have a need to be needed but, at the same time, the selfish side of me is grateful that I am free of grandparent duties so I can pursue my own interests before I get too old. I have a natural affinity with children and young people, but one of my hobbies involves youth work, so I find that a comfort. My father's lineage will die out with my daughters but perhaps these issues are just ego driven, a need to see the continuance of a genetic line in order to mark my own existence, or to recognise a physical resemblance in a new generation. I refuse to see this as a loss. Joy.

★

Linda's youthful ambition was to buy a camper van and travel. When she married in her twenties, Linda and her husband promised each other that one day they would set off to unknown destinations with their children. Sadly, finances and practical commitments did not allow this dream to come to fruition and the children have long ago grown up and set up their own homes and families. Linda is still determined that when they retire in the near future the two of them will let their house and drive around Europe.

Some ambitions need to be abandoned, some stay constant despite changed circumstances, and some need to adapt; the trick is to discern the difference.

★

I had always imagined I would marry and have children. In particular I saw myself with a daughter. As it worked out, I never met the right woman and I have stayed single. On a few occasions I have found tears in my eyes when I am walking on the street and I see a father with his little girl. I am in my seventies now, and I find myself seeking out and enjoying the platonic company of women who are of an age when they could be the daughter I never had. Stephen.

★

Patrick had held every intention of going places in his management career, when his wife developed a chronic illness and became physically incapacitated. With two young boys to bring up, he realised his plans had to change. He downgraded his job to one where he could work from nine to five with no overtime expected, and he was home to cook his children's supper after school each day. It has been very different from how Patrick saw his life going, but the demands of being a carer and providing emotional and practical stability for his family overtook his original priorities. The boys are now fully fledged and independent, but Patrick has no regrets in respect of his working life and has learned the art of contentment with what is rather than what might have been.

Many years ago, Janice had a casual lunch party for four friends. They were all full-time mothers married to successful high earners, with the exception of one woman whose husband had money worries with his business. The rest had reasonably steady lives and predictably stable futures.

Since that time the person who did not see financial security ahead and who complained about the state of her marriage at that time has, as it turns out, had the most straightforward existence. Her husband sold the company which was causing him problems, they moved to an area where the housing was cheaper and jointly set up a less stressful small business which is still flourishing. Nowadays they are living a life of comparative tranquillity and ease. For the others, one was widowed, two went through a divorce and one now works to support her husband who suffers from ill health.

All of the women are coping well, and Janice tells this not as a tale of tragedy and woe but as a tale of life.

★

Although I foresaw working part-time for the sake of fulfilment, I never wanted to be a career woman. I was brought up by a mother who was a full-time housewife and who was always at home for me and my brothers. We lived in a

spacious house with a swimming pool and a tennis court. At the time I was not
aware of how privileged my upbringing was and I assumed my life would follow
this pattern. Unlike my father, though, the man I fell in love with is not in the
high-earning professions. My husband is creative, kind, thoughtful, and a
wonderful and loving husband and father, but because he is self-employed his
income is unpredictable. As a result I have to work to provide a steady and
dependable salary we can rely on and at first I counted this change of outcome as
a loss. Luckily I have now altered my outlook completely and am excited about
challenging myself in career terms. We cannot afford to buy our own house so we
rent, and we live very simply. Apart from ever-present financial pressures, we
are very happy. It might not be the life I would have predicted, but I have learned
a lot, grown a lot, and although I would love not to worry so much about money,
on the whole I would not change how things have turned out. Hannah.

★

It is not all about ourselves though. Dreams and aspirations
can be for those we love, especially our children.

Some parents have specific expectations of how their
children's lives should develop but perhaps most of us just
want our children to be happy, settled and secure. Even that
is a tall order in a precarious and mercurial world, and one
which opens up the possibility of lost dreams.

Almost without exception we aspire to have a loving
relationship with our children when they grow up. What else
is all the hard work of parenting about if this is not so?
Nevertheless, I can bring to mind several families where for
one reason or another they have drifted apart or have failed
to remain as close as they had hoped.

★

My relationship with my daughter has always been of special importance to
me. Possibly because of a lack of love in my own childhood I was determined

to be always there for my own child and being a good parent was fundamental to who I was. When my daughter was undergoing a crisis in her marriage she turned on me in a vitriolic outburst which seemed to come from nowhere. I was incredibly hurt and distressed and the accusations did not make sense and seemed totally unjustified. Although her life is now back on an even keel, she refuses to talk to me about what she said or why she said it. I have tried several times to discuss it with her and to put closure on the whole thing, but she will not even let me bring it into the conversation. I can see that this rejection by her mirrors the pain of my upbringing and that perhaps my feelings are deeper than they would be for others, but I am finding it difficult to trust my daughter and to re-establish our close mother-daughter bond. The loss of this is indescribably sad for me. Wendy.

★

Watching our offspring, of whatever age, experience difficulties and hurt in their lives is extremely painful. It is natural for us to wish for a smooth path for those we brought into the world. The reality can be very different, and the loss of such an ideal can be distressing.

★

Attending a talk for aspiring writers some years ago, the speaker, a well- known radio and television presenter and an author of considerable merit, assured his audience that we need not look far for something worthy of a book. He told us we could stop anyone in any street, anywhere, and they would have a story to tell.

I am sure he was right, but for ourselves what we must not do is to get caught up in our own life story as if it were a drama or a tragedy. We must untangle those threads of how we thought it would be before they strangle us, and we must get on with how it is.

As the psychiatrist and author M. Scott Peck advises in his seminal book, *The Road Less Travelled*, living in truth and reality is essential for positive mental health.

★

Since my ex-partner, Greg, decided family life was not for him when our son was five months old, I am acutely aware of the loss of a father figure for Tommy. Not only does he not have a male role model because Greg has chosen not to keep in touch, but I have no one with whom to share the parenting experience, no one to rejoice with over his first words, his first steps, or his first day at school. Greg and I had known each other for many years before we started a relationship so our being together was not a casual affair. I did not intend getting pregnant when I did but I believed it was real love and we would marry one day anyway and have a family together. I feel guilty that I have brought this situation about for my son. I lost the life and the love I had hoped for my future, and I lost my trust in men and in my ability to choose the right person to be with. It has taken seven hard years of struggle to deal with this loss of confidence but I think I am getting there now. The loss of a father figure for Tommy will be harder, and he will have to work through it too when he grows up. It is not how I thought it would be but I am determined to make something of my life, and of Tommy's. Kate.

★

Any time of reflection, whether we are young or old, invites us to look at what it is we really, really want in our lives and at what we have.

To do this we not only need to be scrupulously honest with ourselves, but also to have both the skills of a surgeon and the courage of his or her patient who lies on the table below. We are both people simultaneously.

With the scalpel raised, what of our "how we thought it would be" will we cut out as no longer necessary or realistic?

Which unfulfilled dream no longer serves us well and should be excoriated? Which unrealised hope could become toxic and must be lanced? And what should remain as healthy tissue which has the potential to nurture and feed our future existence if we let it?

If aspirations are only thoughts and have no substance, how wise is it to let those that are unrealised cause us sadness? Stubbornly holding on to an idealised concept of our lives when it is past its sell by date means we exist in the shadow of a fantasy.

We are responsible for our thoughts and we can choose to let them go before they chip away at our soul. What was, was. What is, is. It is the "is-ness" of life on which we need to focus.

Our future is dependent on who we are now so if, today, we find a way to open our loss box and start to let go of redundant dreams, our tomorrow can be less burdened with past hurts. We have a choice.

Unhappiness is the gap between expectation and reality.

Krishnamurti

EXERCISE 2

This is an adaptation of an exercise I did as a psychology student and which I have found to be useful. This process should not be rushed, so allow plenty of time for the thoughts to emerge.

1. Draw a large thought bubble. Note that this is merely a bubble; it has no solidity. Within the bubble write words which encapsulate how you saw your future when you were young. These can be specific goals or more nebulous circumstances or emotions. How did you think life would be? (For example: Engineer. Much travelled. Accomplished pianist. Sporty. Parent of four children. Author. Easy going. Creative. Physically attractive to opposite sex. Comfortably off. Living in France. Happy. Good marriage. Fulfilled. Recognised for my abilities).
2. Dare to be honest with yourself.
3. When you have completed step one, on another page draw a large, square, no-nonsense reality box. This is the "what is" page hence the straight lines and firm structure. What from the thought bubble has come to fruition? Transfer it/them into the reality box.
4. Also in the reality box jot down additional achievements, attainments, circumstances or emotions representing your current situation, positive and negative. Write it as it is.
5. On a third page draw a large cloud. Note that, like the thought bubble in step one, this cloud which represents our tomorrows is not firm. Its shape may change according to the wind and weather. From the original

thought bubble transfer to the cloud any hopes or intentions which have not been realised but to which you still aspire. These can be practical or emotional aims. Also carry over to the cloud anything from the reality box which you would like to continue into your future. Add additional hopes, aims, circumstances or emotions which you would invite into your life yet to come.

6. Underline in blue any leftover content in the first page (thought bubble) which has not become a reality but which is no longer desirable or relevant, and which can therefore be discarded.

7. Underline in red anything in the thought bubble or the reality box which has caused or is causing you pain, sadness, regret or disappointment.

8. Underline in green any residual content which could be recycled and brought forward more positively into the future "cloud". These can include those areas which have not worked out or which are no longer applicable in their original form, but from which something can be salvaged.

In my workshops I encourage participants to write any lingering but unproductive detritus (as in steps 6, 7 or 8) on sticky labels, adding any emotions that go with them if they wish. These are then adhered to a print out of a rubbish bin or a recycling box depending on whether the loss needs to be disposed of permanently or if it can be reconstituted into something more helpful. The most popular conclusion to this exercise is that the picture of the rubbish bin is later set alight in a safe environment, and that the drawing of the recycling box is shredded and composted.

For those who need a more overtly physical means of riddance, we might use small tie labels which are attached to individual balloons and released into the air by each person privately.

Others tie the labels around small sticks or twigs. For those who have an open fire the stick, the loss and any accompanying sadness can go up in flames. For those without a fire, I suggest the participant takes a special trip to a river or fast-flowing stream where both the twig and the loss are carried away downstream with the current.

I am a great believer in ritual and ceremony, so I recommend the above methods of disposal are not done willy-nilly. Find someone who is sympathetic to your intentions and with whom you can share the process, or if you are happy to do it alone, be sure to make it a deliberate, special and thoughtful action. Put time aside to carry out the action of disposal and release.

Whilst this process has a serious intention behind it, remember also to keep it light where you can. Finding humour where appropriate is healing, forgiveness and acceptance are both essential, and including an air of celebration in the decision to move on is helpful.

CHAPTER FOUR

Relationships

There is a tremendous amount of wear and tear on our being when we come into contact with others. We become mentally and psychologically exhausted. We are prone to envy, anger, pride, jealousy, greed, attachment, disappointment, frustration and unhappiness… Our soul becomes wounded, so we need to heal our soul…

Satish Kumar

A shopkeeper's day would be easier if he did not have to deal with awkward customers, and a doctor's if he was not presented with sick patients. An air steward would have a relaxed flight if his job did not include placating travel-weary fliers and a waiter would be stress-free if he was not confronted with hungry diners.

Jean-Paul Sartre is quoted as saying "hell is other people", which most of us would consider a rather dramatic overstatement, but whilst the lone farmer who deals with crops or livestock can largely avoid daily interaction with fellow humans, for the rest of us it is part of our daily agenda.

If association with people on a non-attachment level can be challenging, how do we survive close relationships?

Bearing the scars of lost love, friendship or family ties does not set us apart from the majority. On the contrary, it would be hard to live adventurously and not meet with such loss.

Even with those relationships which work for us, there is necessarily a degree of loss involved. With each serious commitment we make to another, be it a long-term relationship, a marriage, or the birth of a child, we are required to balance the physical, mental and emotional needs of the other against our own. This requires us to surrender or lose some degree of our self-will and self-determination, and to take a step back from that place where we, and our desires, are central.

In these instances we lose in order to achieve a quality of life we deem more valuable, but that does not mean it is easy or that it always goes swimmingly.

Along with the Satish Kumar quote above, I find the words of the author, Melody Beattie, comforting when she tells her readers they "can reasonably expect conflicts of need and the clashing of issues to occur in the most loving, healthy relationships". She writes that such problems are just "one of the cycles of love, friendship, and family."

The reason I have found this particularly reassuring is because I was brought up in an environment where naturally occurring disharmony or unpleasantness was covered up or suppressed. I cannot remember hearing my parents argue, and they rarely raised their voices to my sibling or me. As a result I have not learned to deal with conflict effectively and my instinct is still to run for the hills, which, of course, solves nothing. When even minor troubles occur in my relationships, I have a hard time convincing myself it is not a cataclysmic catastrophe.

My unrealistically high expectations of a peaceful co-existence create loss.

★

Perhaps it is because most of us are social animals who are not made to be alone, that it is in the areas of love, marriage, family and friendship that many of those I have spoken to have expressed an enduring and deep sense of loss.

Romantic love is an area where we can easily lose ourselves and our perspective. I know this because I have lost myself in this way many times, and not just when I was young and naive.

As someone who is strong and independent when unattached, I have been capable of surrendering my sense of self to another when I have been infatuated or "in love". With the years I hope I have learned to overcome this willingness to abandon my autonomy, something which inevitably ends in disaster and loss.

What I can be sure of is that I am not alone in this. When I found the skeletons of old love affairs in my loss box, it was with the certainty that my store of broken hearts, broken promises and broken hopes was familiar to those of us who have been lucky enough to lead rich and interesting lives.

In *The Road Less Travelled* Scott-Peck advises the reader that falling in love is a deception, a trick, to lure us into commitment. He tells us it is nature's way of securing procreation and the future of the species.

The temporary surge of chemicals oxytocin, dopamine and phenylethylamine has been identified by neurobiologists as being responsible for the euphoria of "in-loveness". Our mistake is to think that such a heightened state of being could endure. It appears that by doing so we are setting ourselves up for loss.

The fairy tales our parents read us at bedtime, and which I read to my own children, paved the way for a potential let-down. The prince and princess lived happily ever after partly because their tales of romance did not take into account the washing machine flooding the kitchen floor, someone crashing into their parked car, the lawnmower refusing to start, the hike in mortgage interest, unexpected redundancy or the occasional sense of monotony in daily life. Even Cinders and Prince Charming would be hard pressed to sustain their adoration of one another under these circumstances.

★

I have always been more passionate about my work than my marriage. I have been married twice but both times this was a challenge for my husbands, who placed themselves in competition with my love for the work I felt was almost a mission. In the end I lost my conditioned belief that marriage was necessary for happiness. I have accepted that the rest of my life will be as a single person. I am happy with the status quo and what I have accomplished in career terms but I am aware of the cost, the loss, to achieve it. Rhoda.

★

As the passion dissipates we may discover what we feel is not even love; we may see it is merely infatuation or good old common or garden lust.

I am amazed at the list of people who, at one time or another, I fooled myself into believing I adored, and surely could not live without. If I met them now, we probably would have nothing to say to each other. That is, if we recognised each other at all.

Much of the stuff of our loss box may be the corpses of these episodes, times when we had convinced ourselves we had found "the one". Is it time to discard these losses?

★

Luckily, the initial stage of romantic love can lead to a more genuine and meaningful relationship, but this requires a heavy duty commitment from both parties to make it work.

As the thrill and novelty fades, this loss of excitement can be compensated for by the calmer love, the deep caring, and the true friendship and companionship that hopefully follows in its wake.

For many of a romantic nature there needs to be letting go of idealism in favour of a more pragmatic approach to love and relationships.

In order to truly love it is necessary to open our hearts to another, to make ourselves vulnerable. We do this in the full knowledge that we may suffer hurt and loss. It takes courage, especially if we have had previous failed relationships, but there is no other way.

If past hurts create a barrier over which our ability to love cannot leap, loss is inevitable. We need to find a way of wiping clean our emotional slates. To love and be loved is a human impulse deeply ingrained in our being and for the majority of us it is worth the risk.

★

Now in his thirties, Eddie had a brief earlier marriage which failed due to his inability to stay faithful to his wife. He has since been going out with Claire for a year and they plan to settle down together and start a family. He admits to missing the potential sexual frisson of meeting someone new and exciting when he socialises but has belatedly realised that this loss is the cost of maintaining a long-term relationship with the woman he loves.

This is no minor loss. When we bind fully to another we necessarily abandon the prospect of those heightened emotional thrills and hormonal rushes experienced in the unchartered waters of new love affairs. This loss is written into the rules of a monogamous relationship. We may flirt in moderation, but if we want the depth and trust of a mature relationship or a marriage, we are compelled to embrace this loss as part of the package. The inability to do so is responsible for many a groaning loss box, and the devastating fall-out from deception and betrayal can result in a degree of loss from which it is hard to move on.

★

In marriage we commit to caring equally for our husband's or wife's well-being, and by doing so we forfeit our right to make life decisions without regard for another. In the words of St Paul, "you are no longer your own". This loss of self-centredness is necessary so we can achieve something more worthwhile.

However much we love our partner or spouse, we would be lacking in individuality if we agreed with them 100% of the time. As covered in the earlier quotes, there are occasions when their need conflicts with ours.

We may want to go out for the evening when they would like to curl up by the fire and watch a film. They may feel like sex when we want to read our book or catch up on sleep.

A husband may prefer to have a stay-at-home partner, but by agreeing to this the wife loses her financial independence and stimulus outside domesticity. A wife may be satisfied with a spouse who earns an average wage and leaves work on time to help put the children to bed, but her husband could lose his chance of a successful career and thereby a sense of achievement by not being willing to put in extra hours.

Getting married is easy, staying married is less so. It is not surprising that many do not make it.

★

I met my husband when I was a fifteen-year-old schoolgirl who had known only a very sheltered upbringing. I married when I was twenty, but after several years of marriage and the arrival of two children, I felt there must be more to life and I left. I now realise I was expecting my husband to give my life purpose whereas, with maturity, I now know I needed to find that for myself. Like most marriages ours was not made in heaven, but we loved each other very deeply and if I had known then what I know now, I am sure we could have made it work. It is easy for me to regret what happened and to beat myself up, but the fact is I did not have the knowledge then, and the wisdom I have gained has come partly from the experience of living without his love. The loss of this relationship is something I have needed to work through later in life, and to let go of in order to enjoy the existence I have built in its place. I am sure my story is one amongst millions. Zara.

★

Bill married for security and not for love. He had an unhappy, lonely childhood with very little affection so when he met Rosie he decided to go along with her suggestion of marriage. Together for nearly thirty years and with two sons, they have been reasonably happy. Bill cares for his wife deeply but has never been particularly physically attracted to her. He has had a couple of short affairs of which Rosie is unaware, so he knows he is capable of passion when the attraction is there. He does not think he would change things now, and he appreciates all that Rosie has provided for him, but he believes he has lost out on love, and on good sex. He is sad that Rosie has lost out too because he knows she deserves someone who loves her in a way he cannot.

Jennifer knows loss by living in what she refers to as a "silken prison". By this she means that her husband's high-earning capacity made it easy for her to stay at home. Whilst her children were young she found this ideal, but now in middle-age she is aware that not being required to develop a career or have work interests outside the home has limited her development. Jennifer's cushioned lifestyle has meant she has lost confidence. She is grateful for the standard of living and security her husband's earnings provided, but she feels unfulfilled and dissatisfied with what she has achieved. Their marriage is happy and one that looks set to last the course, but just as her husband is talking of retiring, Jennifer is looking to break out of her comfortable restraints and challenge herself in the wider world.

★

Marriage has changed beyond recognition over the last fifty years. Feminism has dislodged traditional roles of husband and wife, and most couples now negotiate the sharing of domestic duties and childcare between them. In many ways this had been a great advance, but in others it is a loss.

So many young families struggle under the strain of juggling the responsibilities of home, family and work pressures. The feminist movement was largely about empowering women and giving them choice, but for those women who might prefer to be at home more or be a full-time housewife and mother, the choice is not always there.

Some of the thirty to forty-year-old women I spoke to for this book told me of their experience of loss through the balancing act of motherhood and career. Those who had either opted or been obliged through financial need to follow a career felt they had suffered loss through not being able to give their children more time. Those who had stayed at home sensed they had not only lost their independence but also the respect that a working woman receives. They felt reduced because society did not appear to value the contribution of full-time motherhood.

The loss box is filling up nicely.

I love to see fathers so involved with their babies and children which is a great improvement on the past, and this is surely a gain for everyone involved. Nevertheless, watching young couples it seems their weekends are taken up with shopping and domestic duties and there is little "down" time.

It is certainly more difficult to find the space for regular weekend gatherings of the extended family as used to happen in the past. Whether or not we consider this a loss is an individual matter, but I certainly do.

I would not defend the attitude to women or women's

rights pre-feminism, and I believe strongly in the equality of the sexes, but I am not convinced we have got it right yet.

★

Many of the post-war generation benefitted from rising house prices and have been able to capitalise on these assets to provide for a comfortable retirement. Their gain, however, has been a loss for succeeding generations. It is increasingly difficult for the young to buy their own homes, and the financial pressure from huge borrowings to do so can create an enormous strain on the fabric of the family.

Children suffer when their parents are continually under stress, and otherwise loving relationships can fragment under the load.

The bar has also been raised over the last half century in terms of our expectations of marriage. Higher demands are good as long as they are kept realistic and achievable, otherwise loss is the winner.

Longevity, too, has altered the familial landscape. Whereas we could once expect to be married for thirty to forty years before one partner died, this might now be reasonably extended to fifty to sixty plus. Finding the right partner with whom to share such a lengthy commitment is largely a calculated gamble, hopefully accompanied by strength, determination, good humour and, with luck, a large and generous heart.

For those of us, and I include myself, whose marriages have failed for whatever reason, we need to learn the art of forgiveness for ourselves, others and life. If we do not, we compound the loss.

★

Our biological make-up dictates that most of us want to have children, but when they arrive we have to share our time and attention more widely and by doing so we inevitably lose some of the intimacy with our spouse.

Gone is the impulsive love-making wherever and whenever. Who appreciates the weekend breakfasts in bed, the hours spent reading the Sunday papers, the spur-of-the-moment candlelit dinners at the local Italian until they are lost in the hurly-burly of child-rearing?

Ted remembers with fondness the Sunday morning lie-in ritual of his two young children joining his wife and himself in their big double bed whilst together, week by week, they steadily worked their way through the complete set of Beatrix Potter books. These are wonderful memories for him, but such times were at the expense of the intimate moments the two of them might have shared when they were childless.

Far from the idyllic marketing portrayals of first-time parenthood, the real life scenario is often of constant feeding and nappy changing and perhaps a baby that will not stop crying in the night. It can be of exhaustion, sore breasts, frayed nerves, and black lines under the eyes.

Men may feel sidelined and uninvolved in the early stages of parenting. Many of us of both genders have wondered whether we have done the right thing, and need to be convinced that life will get back to normality in the future. Yes, babies are bundles of joy, but also yes, they are hard work.

The arrival of our first baby heralds a period of adjustment as we come to terms with the loss of life as we have known it. We do get back to normality in time, but it is a new normality; the old one is lost and gone for good.

★

When my fourth child was born the midwife said, "A little boy – just what

you wanted." "How do you know what I wanted?" I cried. I love my four
sons and would not be without any of them, but I longed for a daughter and
am still aware of this loss in my life which has not lessened with time. In fact,
it becomes stronger as I age. Gwen.

★

Children do not come with a rule book which they follow. They do not always behave as we would like them to behave. Their personalities do not always fit easily with ours or with their siblings.

There are times when we continue to love them but we do not like their behaviour very much. It is the same for them, and on occasions they would dearly love to swap us for a new set of parents. If we are strict with them they long for a more indulgent parent. If we are too relaxed they may be envious of a friend whose upbringing provides more structure.

As a mother I know I have made countless mistakes, and certainly if I started again now I would do some things very differently.

Stuffed down deep in my loss box were memories connected to my failings as a mother. I have worked hard at letting these go.

★

The number of those I interviewed who had a sense of loss resulting from their upbringing, demonstrates to what degree we can be affected by how our mothers and fathers coped with parenting.

Whilst I acknowledge the genuine difficulties that stem from these early experiences, I have chosen not to use such tales of resulting loss in this book purely because I did not, in the end, feel they were appropriate for the less deep-rooted exercise we are undertaking here. Serious physical, mental or emotional harm in a person's upbringing is beyond the subject with which we are dealing.

★

My husband left me for another woman when our son, Sam, was in his mid-teens. Sam and I had always been very close and I was aware that, especially at this time of his life and as an only child, I had to be careful not to hang on to him for my own reasons. I tried hard to give the message that he need not take responsibility for my happiness just because his father had gone. As far as possible I concealed my sadness and plunged into practical self-reliance. My sense now is of having tried too hard. Perhaps I came across as too capable because now that he has grown up and left home, he seems to be unconcerned about my welfare, scarcely bothering to contact me after a recent minor operation. He treats me with little consideration – as if I were indestructible – and he frequently lets me down when we have an arrangement, again as if I can cope. My husband had a difficult relationship with his mother and this may have influenced Sam. However, whatever the reason, I feel loss both for the closeness we once had and for the way I imagined our adult relationship might be. Wendy.

★

For most people the adage that all parents do their best is applicable. Their best may not seem good enough to the offspring, but we can only do what we can do, and with what we know at the time. If there is such a thing as the perfect parent or parent/child relationship, I have not come across him/her or it as yet. If we expect to be faultless parents, or have faultless children, we will know the meaning of loss.

When we volunteered for family life, did we foresee children who would have the capacity to squabble from morning to night if they so decide? Did we predict teenagers who would spend hours locked in the bathroom only to emerge with hair coloured and tweaked to within an inch of its life? Did we sign up to keep loving young people whose only response to a question is a stifled grunt, but who can nevertheless find words when they need an advance on their pocket money?

It is natural to have hopes for our children. We want them to do well at school. We want them to find good jobs, have financial security, marry a nice person we can get on with, and provide us with healthy, happy grandchildren. Sometimes they can become the repository for our hopes and dreams; perhaps we unconsciously want them to live the life we did not achieve.

Our offspring, however, are their own people. With a great deal of luck our monosyllabic teenagers metamorphose into reasonable adults who hopefully have the confidence to live their own lives regardless of what ideas we have for them.

The potential for conflict within families is a natural result of these tensions, and yet we are lead to believe we should be happy all the time. Such idealistic hopes for an untrammelled family life can lead us to an exaggerated sense of loss when things don't work out according to plan.

And finally, if we have leapt all these hurdles successfully, our children grow up and leave. We recover our freedom but partly lose our role as a parent and our routine family existence as we have come to know it.

Brenda and Michael have two daughters. Nancy, thirty-four, is living in Japan with her husband, Jack, and their twins. Jack was made redundant two years ago and the only suitable post he could find was in Tokyo. They are not sure how long they will be away.

The younger daughter, Stephanie, was sent to New York by her international employers, where she fell in love with an American. Married and expecting her third child, she now lives in Massachusetts.

Is it any wonder our loss box is full?

★

We have never been financially well off but we worked hard to provide our son with a first-class education. He did very well at school, went to university and then moved away from our hometown to further his career. He has married into a family which, whilst not wealthy, has more money by far than ours, and they come from a grander background. In many ways his in-laws have become his parents too because he probably has more in common with them now than with us. We encouraged our much loved son to achieve and to succeed beyond what would have been expected in our neck of the woods, but we have lost him as a result. We do not regret what we did for him, but we miss him in our lives. Marion.

★

What did we hope for our relationships with siblings, if we have them? Did we expect them to be a large part of our lives?

The personalities of some brothers and sisters are compatible whilst others clash. The former may remain close in adulthood whilst the latter are less likely to be involved with one another, or they may break away entirely.

It is possible for siblings to be so different that it is hard to believe they come from the same stock. Children who were reared and nurtured more or less identically, brought up with the same values, may still mature into polar opposite characters.

There are no rules about sibling affection; there is no right or wrong. Sometimes it works wonderfully well, sometimes it does not. They may be our best friends; alternatively, we may love them but not like them much. Or we may love and like them, but still struggle to find common ground on which to connect.

Even if we have a good relationship with our blood relatives, what happens if we find it less easy to like their choice of partner?

What do we do if we do not approve of the way they bring up their children?

Acceptance of differences is essential if we are to keep the love alive. Family dynamics are set up for loss and, yet again, unrealistic expectations can be the culprit.

★

Coming home today, I found a message on the landline from a very dear friend. Linda had called for no reason other than to say hello and to send me a loving message.

Squeezed between the shopping list and the to-do list on my fridge door is a magnetised quote which reads "friends are the family we choose for ourselves".

The feeling of warmth and comfort Linda engendered in me with her familiar voice and her kind words is living proof of that sentiment. We are related through shared interests, mutual acceptance and deep affection.

My parents, and my mother in particular, did not seem to need close friendships, so I grew up without understanding their true value. I am not sure if this was just an idiosyncrasy of my family or if it was typical of their generation to be so self-sufficient.

Following their example, I did not bother to keep in touch with school friends, and as we moved houses and areas quite regularly these relationships were necessarily impermanent and comparatively superficial. It was not until my thirties that I started collecting special people into my life, and now I wonder how I would cope without my "family" of friends.

In friendship we are drawn to our mirror image, whether the reflection is of a life situation, interests or personality. It is through these relationships that we learn about ourselves and our ego, or sense of self, is reinforced. There are, though, times when even the deepest friendships can falter. If, for example, one person enters a committed relationship or becomes a parent before his or her friend, the shared values and interests can dissipate either temporarily or permanently.

★

I met Jenny at the open day of my college. She was living in South London at the time but she was planning to move to Germany with her husband during the first year of the course. Within about an hour of meeting her it was agreed that she could live with us part-time so she could continue her studies. She moved in and quickly became very much part of our lives. After she qualified she decided to move back to her homeland – New Zealand. I cannot face the long flight out there to visit, and although I expect she will come back now and again, our close friendship cannot remain the same at that distance. I really miss her and it was a great loss when she moved away. Linda.

★

However much people care for one another, it is possible to outgrow a friendship. The unexpected in life can take any one of us in new directions, and such twists and turns may result in leaving behind those you love.

It seems to me there are four main types of friendship:

There are "people we know". These good acquaintances can include work colleagues, neighbours, people we see regularly in a club, community, exercise class or other gathering. They are people we like but our connection with them remains within the shared setting. The capacity for loss here is limited.

There are "path friends". These are people with whom we

walk for however long our paths merge through shared experiences.

When my children were young I remember getting together with others who were going through a similar stage. We could discuss concerns over nappy training, complain to one another about lack of sleep, provide support and comfort where needed. These friendships served me well; in fact I would go so far as to say they were a lifeline. The bond did not always stay the course, however, once the common denominator of early parenting was no longer relevant, and gradually much of the contact lessened and eventually ceased. This is not to dismiss the importance of our shared times, or to question the sincerity of the togetherness whilst it lasted.

I know people who have got together with fellow sufferers during a period of grief, at the end of a broken relationship, or other of life's challenges. Friendships where each helps the other to overcome similar difficulties, offer opportunities to communicate at a profound level and can be an enormous source of strength.

It may be that when both parties have made a good recovery the friendship is established enough, and the connections sufficiently strong for the link to develop into something more long-term. On the other hand, it may come to a natural end without too great a loss.

★

I lost my best friend. We met when we were in our early thirties, and both of us were single parents. We had so much in common, we saw each other at least once a week, went on holiday together with our children, and shared our innermost feelings with one another. We joked about going on the internet to meet new partners but, unlike me, she actually went ahead and did it. When she told me she had fallen for somebody I was devastated. I know it is not logical or rational but I felt betrayed, as though she had been unfaithful to me or to our friendship. They have been living together for nearly three years now, and are talking about getting married. She and I meet now and again but it is not the same. I am still grieving for what we once had. Deborah.

★

The third category is the "good friend". These affectionate friendships can last a lifetime or they can exist for a finite period. Good friends may travel side by side for a while before reaching a crossroads where they find themselves taking diverse paths, or they may drift off only to return later. Alternatively the bond can remain more constant but the intensity may vary over the years.

As we mature, our personalities and our attitude to life can change with the diverse influences we encounter and the choices we make. To expect friendships, even good ones, to last indefinitely is a tall order. It may be we unknowingly have something to give which will help in each other's development, and when our job is done it is time to move on.

I have learned so much that has been beneficial from good friends, not necessarily with their conscious knowledge but often merely by their example. It would not be an exaggeration to say that some have been "teachers", as if sent by grace.

Losing a close friend can be a very real sadness. Recently a long-standing friendship of mine petered away due to life changes which took us in different directions. I am, however, determined not to put this in my loss box. Instead, I will remember the ad hoc get-togethers, the bring-and-share meals, the many glasses of wine, the laughter and the tears over twenty or so years and I will be grateful.

Good friends are one of life's essentials. If they are long-term we will have the richness of shared history. Perhaps they knew us when we were young, or our children when they were babies. We will have seen each other in good times and bad. We will have been there for each other when we needed help. The relationship may not see us into the sunset but the merit of good friendships far outweighs any potential for loss.

★

My husband and I have always worked together running our own business. We are lucky enough to have a strong marriage, and I would not change the circumstances of my life. I am, however, very aware that our togetherness has been at the expense of my being able to make a social life of my own, especially female friendships. From time to time I still see friends from my youth, but rarely on my own. Friendships which have come about since my marriage are shared, and are mostly with couples, which is lovely but they are not the same and they cannot have the intimacy that close friendships between women often have. Men and women talk about different things and I would love to have some really good friends nearby that I could meet up with regularly. I am conscious this is a loss. Joan.

★

Leaving the best to last, the crème de la crème of friendships is the soulmate, or "friend of the bosom" as someone I know refers to them. These are the stuff of life, the people to whom we can bare our soul (hence "soulmate"), holding nothing back, and with whom we feel utterly safe.

Such friendships rise above the ego and corrosive emotions such as envy or jealousy. These are the persons who are privy to our innermost thoughts, who will tell us as it is, but kindly. They may not approve of all we do but they will not judge. These people genuinely want the best for us; they will support us through thick and thin; they will love and nourish us, and we will reciprocate the honour.

Soulmates are pure gold and they are few. In my life, other

than the love I bear for my children and grandchildren, I have found these rare relationships to be the purest and most unselfish form of love. Occasionally, with these friends, I have touched holy ground.

Although the loss of a deep friendship for any reason has the potential to be devastating, just as with a romantic relationship, a marriage or partnership, there is no way to be fully alive other than to open our hearts when such a gift is presented to us.

★

Not included in this list, but possibly the most important relationship of all, is that which we have with ourselves.

In many self-help manuals we are urged to love ourselves. To me this sentiment seems rather trite and simplistic even though I can see it is valid. Changing the terminology but not the sentiment, I prefer the more down-to-earth advice that we need to be our own best friend.

In this traditionally Christian influenced culture we are conditioned to think of others before ourselves as the right way to live, despite the fact that the Bible records Jesus as inviting us to love our neighbours "as" ourselves. As far as I am aware, there is nowhere He said "more than".

My interpretation of this advice is that rather than put ourselves at the bottom of the list as we are often taught, we should show ourselves regard first and foremost, and that by doing so we set the standard to treat others well too.

I have been a bit slow on the uptake on this score, but I have now come to believe our relationships with others start with that which we have with ourselves, and in practice I have found this approach works better than the other way round.

If we can face ourselves, accept and understand our weaknesses, flaws, strengths and gifts, if we offer ourselves the forgiveness and compassion we would extend to our dearest friend, we build an emotionally stable, healthy base from which we are able to love and care for others.

This self-acceptance and compassion does not mean we give ourselves carte blanche to behave badly, far from it, but being over critical or indulging in self-flagellation has no place either. If we lose love and respect for ourselves, if we do not give enough time to that singular relationship, we lose something beyond worth, not by accident but by neglect.

It is from this well of self-regard and self-care that all else springs, and in this way we can see that such self-focused attention is not so much selfish as selfless.

Oscar Wilde wrote that "to love oneself is the beginning of a lifelong romance." We all need some romance in our lives so, if loss of friendship with yourself is in your loss box, take it out right now and set in motion a means to reconnect. Metaphorically wrap your arms around your heart and start the healing process. Be your own best, most loving friend.

I became convinced that the only task in the life of each individual consists in strengthening love in himself, and in doing that, transmitting it to others and strengthening love in them also.
Lev Nikolayevich Tolstoy

EXERCISE 3

When I moved into a new house some years after the break-up of a long relationship, my ex-partner kindly gave me a jasmine for my garden. After a shaky start, the plant gradually took root and thrived. I never felt completely happy with its presence, though, because it seemed to be a reminder of a period in my life which had been difficult.

Each winter the leaves of the jasmine dropped, and each spring it blossomed again. This year, however, it appeared to have given up the ghost. I cut it right back and waited. Nothing happened. Eventually I tried to dig up the roots but it resisted, and then I caught sight of minute signs of new growth coming from the bowels of the earth. I replaced the soil around the stem and fed it. The green shoots are now clearly visible in the flowerbed and the plant has been granted a second life.

When I thought the jasmine was dead there was a part of me which was quite pleased. If it had represented unhappy memories of loss perhaps I could now let it, and them, go. When it fought back and was obviously determined to survive I had to change that attitude of mind. I decided to help it to re-grow, but on my terms. It would flourish with my care and attention but it would not be allowed to hold the hurts it had previously symbolised; I had taken control of its presence.

Flowers are involved in the following exercise which I use in my workshops and which demonstrates one way I have dealt, and continue to deal, with my losses. I will explain how it helps me in the hope that if it seems appropriate, you can use it in some form for yourself, either in a group setting or individually.

I am no artist (in fact my small grandchildren are better at drawing than me!) but that does not matter. I have deliberately produced my own drawings to prove that the quality of our efforts is irrelevant; it is the emotional content that is of value. The illustration is of a flowerbed and this is how it works for me.

Each plant represents something meaningful, and there is a blend of loss, growth and new beginnings. My life starts on the left-hand side and works up to my present on the right. There are a few coloured flowers in my early days but the majority have withered and died. None have grown very high. This is because I found much of my childhood difficult. I also spent a large part of my youth feeling lost, deeply inadequate, different and alone. I can look at that young girl now and feel compassion; I want to put my arms around her.

The first two tall plants are my marriages. The largest and brightest blooms on these are the children from the relationships. Very few marriages are all bad so the plants contain both coloured flowers and some that have died and turned brown, representing the positive and negative aspects, and my struggles during those times. The third tall plant is my own personal growth later in life, and although there are a couple of dead heads, it is mostly colourful and in bloom. In between and amongst these three plants there are small shoots, some of which endured and flourished which represent friendships, interests and achievements, and some that failed to take root – relationships, lost dreams and hopes that withered. Some plants, however, have thrived and are climbing high and spreading new shoots. Many of these are developments which have helped me to progress.

There have been dry periods in the life-long creation of this flowerbed when growth has been impossible and survival is all that could be expected. There have been times of abundance, rain and sunshine. There have been seasons of colour and no colour. In some places, there are patches of stones in the earth which have determined that only the hardiest plants could make it through; but perhaps those stones have also retained water or helped to protect the plant roots, and have therefore been beneficial for what lies in wait.

If a flowerbed represents our life story, and each plant an ingredient within it, we need to work out what we will prune, cut back or discard. We also need to decide which plants to feed and nurture so they will be there for our future.

Without rush or hurry we can gently cut out a plant which is no longer appropriate or healthy, and the memory of which is damaging to our well-being. We can cut each stem into small pieces and put it in an imaginary compost bin where over time it will dissolve into a source of rich soil in years to come. We can allow time for that disintegration process to be completed before we move on to the next plant. We will handle each with thoughtfulness and care.

This illustration could equally be used for the different chapters of this book, each one focusing on a specific area of our lives and deserving of a flowerbed in its own right.

It might also be helpful to create an ongoing flowerbed where we can record our good and bad experiences, and those that hurt us, as they happen. In this way our loss box becomes redundant.

CHAPTER FIVE

Who We Are

Truth is within ourselves; it takes no rise from outward things,
whate'er you may believe.

Robert Browning

Each time my daughter visited me when her children were young, we had a silly routine. I answered the bell by calling, "Who is there?"

"It's me," her then three-year-old son replied.

"Who are you?" I asked as I unlocked the front door.

"Me," he repeated each time.

How wonderful to know that one is "Me" without any labels. Unfortunately this simplicity does not suffice as we grow up. It is natural for each of us to build an image of ourselves to present to the world; without it we may feel we are nothing. The image, however, is just what it says; it is a picture in the imagination. It is created by the mind; it is not the real thing.

I, for example, am a woman, a mother, a grandmother, a Quaker, white, British, a senior citizen, a divorcee, a writer, a life coach, a workshop facilitator and the owner of a small business. It is true that I am all of those things, but is it who I am? Is that all of me? Is that the essence of my being? If, as many believe, we are born over and over again, what of you or me would be reborn each time?

Who we are is a complex question. The nineteenth century American philosopher and psychologist, William James, is quoted as saying "For God's sake, choose a self and stand by it" but that is not as easy as it first appears. Finding out who we are can involve a lifetime's search.

The same grandchild mentioned previously has now started full-time school. Already he is being influenced in his behaviour and his choices, by others. Predictably he has lost the blind sureness of who he is. Like the majority of us he wants to fit in and has adopted some of the language, attitudes, likes and dislikes of his new found friends. It is hard to withstand the pressures to be one of the crowd.

Even as adults we can be affected by the company we keep, and strength of character and intelligence are not always sufficient to protect us.

★

For many of us life may be a series of becoming and unbecoming, or as William Shakespeare puts it, "one man in his life plays many parts." Our lives, for a variety of reasons, might be fragmented, full of flux and change; so much so that we can look back on the vastly different chapters as personal incarnations and see we were different people at different times.

These incarnations can dictate which aspects of our person we present on any one occasion. We may find ourselves adapting to the current company according to which stage of our life he, she or they represent, and so which incarnation is relevant to the relationship.

This does not mean there is no integrity in who we are; hopefully we are completely sincere and true to ourselves in each case. It is just that what that particular person or those persons know of us and what we have in common is what is brought to the fore.

In many ways, each mini-lifetime, or incarnation, has been a loss. One embodiment must largely die to allow the next to emerge. Each time we have taken with us the distillation of who we are, but the surface wrapping is no longer representative in its totality and to one degree or another must be discarded.

★

I moved to the UK well over twenty years ago when I was in my thirties and am very happy here. What I am confused about, though, is where I call home. Is it where I was brought up and went to school, where my childhood friends still are and my family roots? Or is it here, in England, where a large chunk of my married life has been and where my child was educated? I have lost sureness in my sense of belonging. Petra.

★

Hannah underwent chemotherapy for an aggressive form of cancer, uncertain of whether or not she had a future. When the treatment was over and she was eventually given the all clear, she faced the daunting task of rebuilding her life. Having been forced to stare death in the face she emerged as a distinctly different person. Hannah went into a deep decline when she realised she no longer had the closeness she had previously known with some former friends. It was not that they had fallen out; it was simply that she had changed. Hannah did not have the same outlook on life as prior to the illness. She was no longer driven to work long hours and much of her spare time was now devoted to working for a local charity which supports other cancer sufferers. It has taken several years for her to let go of old ties and in many ways she has found this emotional pain even more difficult to cope with than the medical treatment.

Looking at old photographs, perhaps we can see the distinct people we have been and the separate lives we have

lived within the one life. It may well be there are others yet
to come.

★

*The need for religion was in me from early childhood, but I lost my faith in
adulthood. This left an enormous hole in my life and for a while it
undermined the reason for my existence and confidence in knowing who I
was. I am still sad that I can no longer accept something which was so much
a part of my upbringing, but it is impossible to deny it when something no
longer fits. I am not the person I was then. Steve.*

★

When her youngest child left home to get married, Ginna felt
she had to release her identity as a mother. Of course she
remains a mother in a biological definition forever because
she gave birth to her children, but her nurturing role in terms
of bringing up her children to go out into the world was
complete. She had lost that part of who she was. It has taken
several years of grieving to come to terms with this loss but
finally Ginna accepts she is still the same person she ever was;
her core being remains.

In midlife I had some success in writing feature articles
for newspapers. I worked as a freelance and at first I was lucky
enough to sell almost every piece of work I produced. It was
a labour of love, it gave me a sense of purpose and I began to
consider myself a "professional" writer. When the internet
encroached on the newspaper industry and market forces
meant cutting back on outside contributions, my market more
or less dried up.

I learned to deal with rejection and eventually I had to let
go of my newly acquired professional image. I had picked up
a new identity and, just as quickly, I lost it. Did that change

the "real me"? No, it did not, but I nevertheless had to go through a period of reluctant readjustment and I know that particular loss landed with an extra heavy thud in my loss box.

Nowadays I quite regularly get together with other writer friends and we produce short stories and poetry just for our pleasure. It does not earn me a title, but I love it all the same and my previous feeling of loss is largely offset.

★

Unlike my brothers who went on to the local grammar school, I failed my eleven plus exam, and my parents scraped the money together to send me to a private school. Nevertheless, I thought of myself as a dunce and I never shone academically; I felt different and just wanted to stay in the background. As a result I had no career aspirations and settled down into marriage, domesticity and child-rearing as soon as the opportunity came along. It is only now, in old age, that I understand my gifts were creative rather than academic. I have always been passionate about colour and texture, and designed and made my own clothes. I did the same for my children when they were young. Also I would buy knitting patterns and play around with the designs to make something unique. If I had been born in today's world where such talents are more recognised, I would have gone into fashion. I have spent most of my life thinking I was useless when in reality I was not a failure at all. I was a budding fashion designer; I just didn't know it. I am so frustrated that I lost the chance to do something I would have loved and a much-needed validation of who I was. Naomi.

★

Many years ago Jeremy, a hitherto impressionable young man, took part in a workshop; he does not even remember what it was about. What he does recall is that, prior to the event starting, those present were asked to write one descriptive word about every other person in the room.

The group was sitting in a circle with a good view of each other, and as far as Jeremy was aware, no one knew any of the others. When the short exercise was over each person was given a sheet of paper with all the adjectives relating to themselves.

His list included resilient, friendly, gentle, severe, reserved, intelligent, kind, serious, intense, open, humorous, outgoing and forbidding. He admits to being all of these on differing occasions but these assessments, some of which were contradictory, were made at exactly the same time when he was in the same mood. How could this be?

Retrospectively he has found the exercise tremendously helpful and has since resolved not to let the opinion of others unduly influence his sense of self, either in terms of compliments or criticism. He does not always succeed in this resolution but change of such an ingrained habit is, by necessity, a work in progress.

Obviously it is nice if people say positive things, and equally he feels a need to examine his faults if they are pointed out, but now he is conscious that others will see him according to their own likes, dislikes, influences, prejudices or life history.

To exist primarily in terms of what others think of us and to rely on a selfhood that comes from such reflection is a risky affair. We are not merely what other people make of us; we are who we are.

Along this line, a saying I particularly love is: "What others think of you is none of your business".

If ever I find myself in a situation where I am conscious of making an impression, I try to repeat this to myself internally. It helps me to be who I am rather than who I feel I should be in present company. It helps me to admit "I don't know" in answer to a question rather than making out I am more knowledgeable than I am. It helps me to say "I don't quite understand" when I am out of my intellectual depth, rather than try to fluff my way through a conversation. This saying frees me up to be myself. There is no pretence, no one is going to "find me out", and therefore there can be no loss.

Just consider how terrifying it must be for those caught up in the artificial world of "celebrity". For some their image is promoted to the status of a "brand", something they or their agents market. If there is not sufficient substance to the image a person or the media presents, their identity, by default, is puff. Those whose identity is puff and air must spend their lives in fear of people wielding pins. Just one prick and all is deflated; all is lost.

Historically, the Japanese culture has been built on "face". The worst thing that could happen to a Japanese man or woman was to lose face. I understand that in this instance "face" encompasses honourable qualities such as integrity and uprightness. To nationalities brought up without this traditional emphasis, however, face in this context means front, or facade. Being careful about such a facade, making sure it is built on solid ground, on the rock of what is real, what is internal and cannot be touched by outside events, can help us avoid loss of self.

★

When I got divorced I lost my position in a world of couples. I still get invited to the occasional social gathering, but I am very much aware that, although I hold a visitor pass, my membership card has been cancelled. Over the years I have recreated a social life but it is mainly with other single women. This is excellent in its way, but I feel a loss of mixed company and of being part of the greater whole. Louise.

★

Sam had the strange sense of having both lost and found himself when he spent an evening experimenting with the art of clowning.

In turn with a group of strangers and a teacher of physical theatre, Sam was asked to don a red nose and enter the room slowly, concentrating only on his breathing. Like everyone present he was instructed not to act or put on any expression but just to stand in the centre of the space facing his fellow participants and to look directly into their eyes, one person at a time. He remembers feeling totally naked, as though everything had been stripped away, and that the mask he normally put on to face the world was not available to him. Sam felt the eyes of others boring into him but at the same time he was aware of receiving only kindness.

It became evident that the red nose was a great leveller because no matter what a person looked like before, no matter what authority he or she commanded, the moment they stretched that elastic over their head and put that nose on, they looked ridiculous.

This exercise helped him to feel connected to who he was, to what was left when the veneer of self-protection and identity he subconsciously erected was taken away. Sam temporarily lost his artificial sense of self but paradoxically found unexpected strength in this very act of disempowerment.

The liberating experience was repeated in reverse when he was in the audience looking at others having the courage to wear the red nose. Their obvious discomfort and vulnerability helped him to see past their persona and into the depths of who they were, evoking a higher than usual level of compassion.

Sam's experience of finding insight by achieving momentary dissolution of the self may have been a glimpse of what Buddhists call "annata", a term for no-self. For those who achieve this elimination of the ego, it follows that there can be no suffering from loss of self esteem or identity. Where there is no ego present there is, quite literally, nothing to lose.

Going beyond "who we are" and adhering to the extreme discipline this state of being requires, however, is likely to be a step too far for the vast majority and we must find other ways to avoid loss.

*

How many women have depended on the admiration of men for self-validation in their youth? I know I did and, surprisingly, the rise of feminism has done little to change this state of affairs. It also seems many young men are adopting a similar attitude to identity as their female counterparts and are becoming more body conscious and concerned with outer appearances.

Taking pride in how we look is great at any age and to be applauded if it is a matter of making the most of who we are. This is especially true when we are celebrating being young and vibrant and we are trying to find a mate. Nevertheless, by continuing to rely too heavily on the transient nature and superficiality of such outward features into adulthood, we may lose the incentive to develop those more long-lasting inner attributes and resources which sustain us in maturity. What happens when our power to attract on a physical level wanes as it surely will? A more rounded sense of who we are and our worth can help us to avoid loss as we age.

*

I was teased unmercifully at school for having bright red hair and inevitably I was nicknamed Ginger, something which remains today. None of this worried me unduly because my parents insisted red hair made me special. I grew it long when I was a teenager, and my "mane", as I called it, became who I was. It made me different and gave me a strong sense of individuality. When I started to go grey early – I was only in my mid-thirties – it was a shock and really difficult to deal with. I was losing something that had become a mark of who I was: the redhead. Now I was just one of the crowd. It was worse for my husband though because he was virtually bald by the time he was forty. We still haven't heard the end of that loss! Hermione (Ginger).

★

Denial is a tool we use to protect ourselves from knowledge we are not ready to face. It can serve a purpose and allow us to accept a situation in our own time. When we remain in a state of denial as a permanent form of escape from reality, however, we can become detached from ourselves and our feelings. Denial may protect us from our pain, but we can lose that vital connection with who we are.

Bridget had a six-year relationship with someone she met at university. Greg was a domineering and controlling person who continually undermined her. Despite family and friends begging her to leave him, Bridget could not seem to break away. Her career suffered and her friendships faltered as she allowed herself to be treated in a way that caused anguish to those who loved her.

Luckily for Bridget she woke up one morning and, inexplicably, felt able to go. She describes her attachment to Greg as being in thrall, as though she had been bewitched. Without warning, the spell was broken and she could see quite clearly what others had been telling her all along. Bridget had misinterpreted Greg's bullying and overpowering nature as strength, and his control as love. She had been in denial about who he was and the effect he was having on her. In doing so she had lost touch with herself, her value and her needs.

★

Work is an area where identity is most powerful. When we go to a party how often are we asked what we do? I am a doctor. I am a computer programmer. I am a homemaker. I am a graphic designer. I am a lawyer, plumber, carpenter, or whatever.

This question is not senseless; it can open up channels for conversation and hopefully the answer is a pointer to what provides that person with some life satisfaction. Knowing another's profession, however, does not mean we have an in-depth insight into who he or she truly is.

What we do for a living and who we are can get confused. Naturally, our work affects us, especially if we are lucky enough to do something about which we are passionate, but it is not the totality of us. It is not who we are. I am, therefore I do, and not I do, therefore I am.

★

For about a ten-year stretch I was trying to earn a living doing a series of jobs I hated. Looking back I can see this made me quite hard which is not my real personality at all. It was as though I had to detach from the sensitive person I am just so I could cope with what I had to do practically, and in order to survive financially and put food on the table. Luckily things have eased a little now, and gradually I have been able to return to being my own person again. It has been a slow realisation of how far I had strayed from "me". I feel sad about those years though because it was as though I lost sight of who I was. Sandra.

★

Meriel's story is an example of how we can get work and identity confused. Meriel had been brought up with a strong work ethic and she had been programmed to achieve. Her career in the Civil Service took her almost to the top of the ladder, but in order to get there she got up at around six o'clock each morning to catch an early train and be at her desk by seven-thirty, arriving home at eight in the evening or later. Weekends were spent on domestic matters and in recovering from the excessive workload.

In her late forties Meriel was made redundant and she was forced to stop and take a fresh look at her life. She had been so busy achieving her goals, so focused on her career, that she had neglected her social life and had not found time to invest in meaningful relationships. Friendships amongst her work colleagues were, by necessity, restricted because of her isolating position of seniority. She had not married or had children, and there was no one to prop her up when she was in trouble.

For Meriel, work had been who she was. It took some time to recover from this loss of identity, but she has since retrained and is now successfully self-employed. Whilst she still has to fight the urge to overwork, she has taken up a hobby through which she has met new people with whom she shares an interest.

Meriel's life is more fulfilling, but she is aware of how much she has lost in the past by her concentration on only one aspect of living. The best outcome of all is that she no longer relies on her work to create who she is or to justify her existence, so that particular loss can come out of her loss box.

Jennifer's story is not dissimilar. She was way past retirement age and each year she swore she would retire, but each year, despite being permanently exhausted, she did not. She said it was because she was concerned about money and that she would miss the stimulus her younger co-workers provided, but maybe there was more to it than that. Perhaps leaving her job meant leaving part of herself behind.

When we go to work and mix with colleagues our identity is reinforced. When we have a title it helps us to know our position in society. Is there a fear that when we let go of our work we will be a non-person?

Jennifer finally took the plunge some months ago, after a stress-related illness. It is now almost impossible to meet up with her because she is so busy doing interesting things, spending time with her grandchildren, taking a course on one subject or another, going to exhibitions, or travelling. She has re-found an identity which is not dependent on anything other than who she is.

★

In my forties I started a business with my husband which is now well established. Twenty years on, our children are managing the company and we have taken a back seat. It is very hard to let go, and although we are pleased to see the next generation continuing what we started, we feel very out of the loop. Their decision-making frequently excludes us, especially when it comes to keeping up with technological advances which they are introducing. We know this is how it should be but the loss is something we constantly have to rationalise. Diana.

★

At the opposite end of the scale is the job which offends our sensibility or which degrades us.

Olaf is a foreign mature student who is trying to pay his way through college, so he can change career. To pay his rent and the high living expenses of surviving in London, he works in the evenings and weekends in a gambling establishment. In addition to casual customers, he witnesses regular punters, those who are playing out their addiction and who are not in control of their gambling habit. It distresses him to be part of this set-up and he continues to look for alternative work that will fit in with his college timetable.

Olaf has to assure himself continually that he is not responsible for the consequences of the behaviour of others and protect himself from being demeaned by his job.

Tying our image of ourselves to our occupation, our work, is a recipe for loss whether we rely on it for supporting our ego, or allow it to restrict what we are capable of achieving.

★

From childhood I longed to be a mother and saw that as my destiny. When I actually became a parent I was shocked to find that I did not enjoy motherhood as much as I had imagined. I love my children but a lot of the time I find being with the kids tedious, boring and frustrating. As being the perfect mum is how I had always seen myself, I am now looking for a new me. Hilly.

★

If our self-worth is too heavily dependent on our career, what happens if we do not get the promotion we applied for? What if we accept an appointment only to find we do not fit in or we cannot meet what is expected of us? What if we are promoted beyond our capabilities or comfort? What if we are made redundant?

Even if we negotiate the world of work without such experiences, there will come a time for all of us when we need to retire. The loss of purpose many people feel when they stop working is legendary. If we have been in a position of power, if what we had to say carried some weight, how do we fill the vacuum created when we no longer have this authority to define us?

When we are taken in by a self-constructed and limiting identity we are likely to rely on it for our self-worth and for our sense of place in the world. If this rug is taken from under our feet we can experience a loss of momentous proportions.

★

In certain circumstances it is possible to lose touch with who we are to dire effect. A spate of inner city riots demonstrated how easily some otherwise rational people could be taken over by the conduct of a crowd and how they were capable of behaving in a way they would not have previously deemed possible. It appears they underwent a process of temporary dissociation.

Many in the banking and financial markets equally lost touch with their common sense in recent years and were seduced by the seemingly acceptable culture of excessive risk-taking. By buying into the madness, they allowed themselves to be led down a path which resulted in chaos and helped to tip much of the world into recession with horrendous consequences, causing great suffering to their fellow men and women.

A number of Members of Parliament, too, felt able to exploit loopholes to behave in ways which would shake the foundation of trust invested in them by the voting public, the same people whose taxes were being misused.

If everybody around us believes what they are doing is acceptable, who are we to question it, to stand apart? If we are repeatedly placed in a climate of rule bending or boundary-breaking behaviour, we may begin to doubt our own judgement. We can become corrupted and lose touch with what we know intrinsically is right or wrong. Rudyard Kipling's poem *If* starts with the words: "If you can keep your head when all about you are losing theirs…". Such a stand requires great strength of character.

Carl Jung, the nineteenth century psychiatrist, psychotherapist, and founder of analytical psychology, wrote of "individuation". Individuation is the process whereby we differentiate ourselves from others and establish a sense of self. It would seem that under particular conditions, this can be eroded to a point where we become, instead, part of a collective, sacrificing our individuation for a state of belonging with the greater whole.

In the above instances, those involved lost their moral compass. It is easy for us to condemn such happenings, but it is likely that we have also strayed from our better selves at some stage, albeit less publicly and hopefully with less drastic outcomes. None of us are immune and at various times in our lives we may find ourselves lost, a stranger to ourselves, and needing to find a way back to our true path.

Unhappy events can lead us down a destructive course of anger, resentment and a desire for revenge where we lose sight of what we know is right. When we judge others who have succumbed to these emotions we need also to ask ourselves if we are capable of similar reactions. The honest answer is likely to be affirmative. There are times when we can become someone we do not like.

★

There was a stage in my youth when I started drinking heavily and behaving irresponsibly. I was a party animal who slept around. I look back on those days with sadness because that was not the real me. I am very different now, and I am not sure why I acted like that. I need to let go of the shame I feel about this period in my life. Maxine.

★

Orthodox Judaism has a special Sabbath between the Jewish New Year and Yom Kippur, The Day of Atonement. Shabbat Shuvah invites those who have strayed in any way from the path of right living to return. Pressured and demanding lives can distract us from our deeper purpose and from following our principles in any or all areas of being. This special Sabbath encourages Jews to address the higher order questions of their purpose in life, their values, and what contribution they have to offer the world. Such a process of "stop and think", and repentance if appropriate, opens up an opportunity and occasion for each person to return to his or her self.

As a non-Catholic I can only assume the confessional offers a similar prompting, but if we truly desire it, this "return to the path" is available to anyone, of any faith or of no faith, who has lost their way. We just have to want it enough.

★

The Loss Box contains a number of references to the writing of Melody Beattie, author of *Co-dependent No More* and other books on co-dependency which I have found invaluable. Some people deride the idea that such a condition exists, but as someone who suffers from co-dependency myself I can assure the reader that it most certainly does.

Co-dependency is partly where a person consistently and repeatedly subjugates or discounts their needs in favour of another's. I will not elaborate in more detail because this is a highly complex subject in its own right, but suffice it to say that unless those of us with co-dependent tendencies address this unhealthy way of living, we are in danger of losing touch with ourselves.

Co-dependants are compulsive fixers. If someone has a problem we imagine it is our responsibility to sort it out regardless of our own well-being, and possibly preventing the person in question from gaining self-esteem by finding the remedy themselves.

My loss box had numerous reminders of times when I neglected myself for the sake of someone else, often unnecessarily, and potentially resulting in resentment on both sides. If you think this might relate to your experience I suggest you investigate co-dependency further and start correcting this imbalance.

There are few people more uncomfortable to be around than a martyr and, as mentioned in Chapter Four, I have rather belatedly discovered that we need to put ourselves high on our list of priorities in order to be able to help others.

★

Holding on to our innermost person through this confusing maze we call life is no mean task, but it is something we need to do if we are to protect ourselves from unnecessary loss.

It is the chiefest point of happiness that a man is willing to be what he is.

Desiderius Erasmus

EXERCISE 4

One of the more madcap exercises I suggest in my workshops is to take a sheet of paper and draw around gingerbread men biscuit cutters of differing sizes. There is some method in my madness because I believe that using childish practices stops us intellectualising or judging what we are trying to achieve and puts us more in touch with our emotions.

These odd looking outlines of people represent who we are or have been at various stages, starting with childhood and adolescence and continuing to the present. These are the ghosts of our past.

In these empty shapes we can write whatever comes to mind. This can include representations of a period in our history such as teenager, university student, trainee, newly-wed, traveller, parent, manager, business owner.

We can add emotions such as fear, passion, vulnerability, confusion, uncertainty and happiness.

We may also wish to make notes of those characteristics present in that particular manifestation. How would we describe ourselves at that stage of our lives? Determined, arrogant, innocent, naive, optimistic, ignorant, enthusiastic, open-hearted, loving, gullible?

The idea is not to flatter ourselves unduly, or to be critical, but to take an objective, honest look at who we were then and to fill the bodies with any relevant words that come into our heads.

When we are confident that all or most of our personifications are represented, we can trace our journey so far. This can be akin to looking down from the gallery at characters on a stage. Some we might like better than others. It may be there is one we could still identify with whilst its neighbour is almost a stranger to us now.

It is possible this process will unmask some losses which would benefit from being released. These may include feelings, roles, status, associations, personality traits or anything else which crops up.

What I normally suggest is we then redraw an outline and transfer all the losses into this. Usually one shape will be sufficient but it can be as many as felt appropriate and we may decide a particular loss demands an outline of its own.

My enthusiasm for ritual makes me recommend that we dispose of this figure as I have suggested before in other exercises, and with definite intention.

If we want to go further, we can redraw yet more body shapes and put in those positive memories we would like to take with us as affirmations of our various embodiments. Perhaps we could also include those attributes which we feel make us who we are, our finer characteristics.

As this work is not intended for serious grief or trauma, try to keep it light where possible and have a gentle, loving laugh at yourself if you can.

CHAPTER SIX

Health

Sooner or later, for those who avoid all conscious grieving, break down – usually with some form of depression – occurs.

John Bowlby

One of the topics I most wanted to cover in this chapter was loss of independence through ill health. The morning I was due to start writing, I tripped and fell, breaking both bones in one ankle and spraining the other. I lay on the floor and wept, not from the pain, although that was considerable, but because I could not see how I would cope with the practicalities of living alone, especially as I have two energetic dogs who need walking daily.

Having undergone surgery to have my ankle pinned, I was then almost entirely confined to my house for over three months. The plastered ankle was not weight-bearing, so I hopped around on the sprained foot with great difficulty, using crutches. Eventually, and much to the surprise of my window cleaner who nearly fell of his ladder at the sight of me, I found it easier to don gardening knee pads and shuffle around on my knees. Obviously I did what I could for myself, but nevertheless I remained more or less dependent on the kindness of others. As a busy, active, independent person, having to ask for help to do even the simplest task was quite shocking.

When my daughter collected me from the fracture clinic and levered me from the wheelchair into her car, she jokingly told me it was good practice for the future. I could see the funny side with her, but my laughter felt hollow – I knew what she said was potentially true and I was horrified.

Luckily for me I am now back on two legs, but after my period of incarceration and disability I will never again underestimate the frustration of others who suffer likewise by losing their mobility and independence through infirmity or merely through old age.

Loss of pride in having to ask favours continuously in order to survive, and loss of autonomy are both lessons that will stay with me indefinitely.

★

In the poet and mystic, Kahlil Gibran's, wonderful book, *The Prophet*, are the words "And ever has it been that love knows not its own depth until the hour of separation".

Anyone who has lost someone close to them will appreciate this wisdom, but the sentiment is not restricted to love. Health and youth are equally taken for granted by most until they are taken from us. Loss of youth applies to everyone, whereas health and its counterpart, ill health, are more random.

★

When I had a breast removed due to cancer, I agreed to an implant to match the other breast and to make things look normal. Five years later it was necessary to remove the remaining breast. Rather than have another implant, I decided the original should be removed. When I was facing the possibility of a terminal illness, being flat-chested did not seem such a great loss in the overall scheme of things and I have grown quite accustomed to it now. Gemma.

★

Tessa was in her late teens when she developed ME. For ten years she rode an energy roller coaster. On some mornings it was virtually impossible for her to get out of bed, she ached all over and her mind felt as though it was wrapped in cotton wool. On other days she managed to go to work for a few hours before she became exhausted. In between these times Tessa would cope well with her job and, as long as she was sensible and did not overstretch herself, she could maintain a reasonable quality of life. What Tessa was unable to do, nevertheless, was make plans; she could not predict how she would be from one moment to the next. Her employers were generous and held her job open for her, but her social life was all but obliterated. She could not party, she dared not do anything too energetic, and her capacity for fun was limited.

Nearing thirty, Tessa found a treatment which worked for her. Since that time she has married and had a child. There is no sign of the illness returning.

Tessa's ongoing sense of loss is that she cannot replace a decade when she should have been footloose and fancy-free. Those were the years when she should have been falling in and out of love, going out and having fun, exploring the world and finding her place in it. She lost out on those rites of passage and those experiences which help to form us over such a time of growth.

★

We are all urged to eat sensibly with a diet that includes "five a day" fruit and vegetables, take regular exercise, drink moderately, give up smoking, and keep our brain cells stimulated. That is not the whole story though, and what we also need are good genes, and a very large dose of luck.

Pat, for example, inherited her mother's genes, which has

meant she suffers from frequent headaches and severe migraines which can leave her incapacitated for several days.

This low-grade ill health has brought loss for Pat in a variety of ways and the condition has got considerably worse with the years. Despite numerous tests, no doctor has been able to pinpoint the cause either in her mother's case or Pat's. One area of loss amongst many that resulted is she has found it difficult to travel. She is so concerned over the potential to have a flare-up whilst she is away that the nervous tension generated by this fear can be a trigger in itself.

★

Sometime in my forties I lost the ability to sleep through the night. I don't want to take sleeping pills so I work with my acupuncturist and other therapists to overcome this problem. I know that lack of sleep has affected my personality as well as my physical health and I am irritable much of the time, so my poor husband and children suffer from my sleeplessness too. Karen.

★

When Sam was told he had a cancerous growth behind his left eye, he thought there was a possibility he would not live to see his two-year-old son grow up, or have the luxury of growing old with his wife. He has now had the eye removed and is recovering well. The experience has quite literally given him a new outlook on life. His remaining eye is struggling to adjust so he occasionally misses door handles and other objects he reaches for, but he is sure that in time he will manage well. His emotional view of his existence has also changed. He is conscious of the loving support he received from those around him whilst he was undergoing treatment, and each day is precious and a gift. He takes nothing for granted.

★

For the vast majority, losing our agility and health is a gradual process with age and many of us learn to cope with increasing aches and pains without it becoming too much of an issue.

I do notice, however, how much more of the conversation between friends is concentrated on this subject as the years go by and it seems this is a loss we need to express and share, even, as is often the case amongst those I mix with, if we turn our moans into something amusing and manage to have a good laugh about it all at our own expense.

A personal example of the normal physical change which is to be expected with increasing age is that having been at full-time ballet school from the age of eight, I can remember being supple enough to jump in the air and land in the splits.

I am not sure how old I was when I lost this level of flexibility, although I remember trying it for a laugh at a particularly drunken party in my thirties. In addition to a well deserved hangover, I could hardly walk for days afterwards. Just the thought of attempting such a thing now is enough to have me dialling the osteopath's number.

★

When I moved from city life to living in a coastal town, I also left behind my job, my home of many years and regular contact with the people who were major players in my life. I taught stress management so I should have been prepared for this all encompassing change to have an impact, even though I thought I was strong enough to cope with the fall-out from most things life threw at me. What happened was I found it gradually more and more difficult to leave the house and eventually I developed full-blown agoraphobia. The panic attacks were terrifying and at times I thought I would die. I had always been an extrovert and enjoyed socialising and giving to others. It took nearly ten years of hard work on my part, hypnosis and other therapies to overcome my fear, and even now I cannot go far from home if I am alone. In some ways I can say I lost those ten years of my life, but in retrospect I can also see that the self-imposed isolation gave me time for deep reflection, reading, and a peace I had not known. I learnt so much that has been valuable to me since. Pauline.

★

Like so many in our society, I have suffered a number of depressive episodes in my life. Some have been for specific reasons such as postnatal blues, the unhappiness and eventual break-up of my second marriage, and the menopause, which mostly manifested as anxiety. This moderate depression with a cause is labelled "reactive depression".

At other times mild depression has appeared stealthily, unbidden, and apparently from nowhere, colouring my world a dingy grey. It is these low periods of what is known as "unspecified depression" that I now relate to my increasing sense of loss.

According to statistics available from the Mental Health Foundation, one in four British adults experience some form of mental health problem in a twelve month period, the most common of which is mixed anxiety and depression. As above, this can be caused by particular circumstances or creep over you like an all enveloping cloud without any obvious trigger, and obscure your view of life.

For me the latter was more disturbing. Depression with a causal stimulus felt more acceptable than a chronic low mood which deemed everything pretty pointless and which appeared for no explicable reason.

Most people have stresses and I know of few without worries of one sort or another, so when I was very low it seemed facile to blame depression on these ubiquitous factors, and hard to justify to those who cared about me and who might be affected by my state of mind.

Depression is a loss for those around the sufferer too. Let's face it, depressed people are not a bundle of laughs and their company can bring others down.

Mental health is not discerning, and a comfortable lifestyle and financial security do not preclude anyone, as we could imagine they might.

Wendy, who is wealthy in the extreme, and who has a loving marriage and family life, could not function if she was not on a permanent regime of antidepressants. On the other hand, Prue, who lives alone and is as poor as a church mouse somehow remains indefatigably buoyant and cheerful. I worry she may suffer a heart attack or a stroke from high blood pressure because she works so hard to pay the bills. She is, however, immune to unhappiness.

★

After the birth of my third child I suffered from postnatal depression which lasted for more than two years. I felt so guilty because I should have been happy with two lovely sons and now this much wanted little baby girl too, but because of the illness I thought I was inadequate and a loser and I had no love to give. I have made a full recovery and I have since established a loving relationship with my daughter, but I still grieve for those lost early years of love and nurture. Claire.

★

I have never experienced the serious depths and darkness of clinical depression for which I am grateful; mine is more of a "what's the point?" variety. It has been what they rather dramatically used to call melancholia in the days of Coleridge or, somewhat dismissively, the glums in the 1940s and 50s.

For Eve, however, the abiding memory she has retained is that depression took the edge off everything. She lost out on joy in all its forms; she could not see the beauty in a flower, or join in with the laughter at a joke. It was hard for her to feel love even for those she cared for deeply, and when she was at her lowest ebb she recalls hiding under the duvet or not feeling able to walk down the street because passers-by might see the big black hole under her ribcage.

Most of the time the illness stayed at a level that allowed her to struggle on and manage on the surface, and not many noticed there was anything wrong. Where possible Eve avoided social gatherings, crossed the road to steer clear of meeting someone she knew, and generally kept her head down.

Not dealing with sadness or depression can result in pain coming out in other ways. Increasingly Eve turned to drink, a short-term remedy that so many people opt for to ease pain. She controlled her intake before she became dependent because she was conscious that too much reliance on any substance or habit could be a road to an even more pernicious loss.

Not everyone, however, is so lucky as to have an inbuilt cut off point with alcohol, and loss through addiction is an area too fraught with potential trauma to cover here. I will add, however, that I have talked to alcoholics who, whilst they cannot get back the years they lost to their habit, have gone on to live happy, fulfilling and worthwhile lives in recovery. As with depression, addiction also involves loss for those who love the sufferer.

For Eve, it took some considerable time initially for her to acknowledge she needed medical intervention for her depression, possibly because she liked to think of herself as strong and found it shameful to admit she wasn't coping. Later, during repeat episodes, she recognised the symptoms in the early stages, and although she still found it hard to ask for help from her GP, she forced herself to seek support without delay.

Eve's remedy was to combine antidepressants with other complimentary therapies such as cranial osteopathy, but there is no "one answer" and each sufferer of depression must find what works for them.

Living life through an unrelenting veil of sadness is not life, it is merely existence. Existing instead of living is loss.

★

Whilst not amounting to depression, it is natural for us all to have times of unhappiness and we need to make space for being down on occasions without feeling there is something wrong or forcing ourselves to snap out it. We need to feel what we need to feel.

Advertisements, especially in women's magazines, are full of smiling, happy individuals. We are presented with television and radio personalities whose grinning faces and chirpy voices would have us believe they do not know the meaning of sorrow.

If we buy into this artificiality, this pastiche, we may believe we are alone in experiencing sadness. The truth is that even if we have everything in place, all our ducks in a row, we are still permitted to experience low times. This beautiful world is also full of suffering, and subscribing to the idea that we should not feel sad can prevent us from admitting to our troubled hearts or sharing our inner turmoil openly and without guilt.

★

Watching your parents' mental and physical abilities gradually diminish is heartbreaking. I have lost my intelligent, independent mother to dementia and my father, who was once so interesting to talk to and who had a wonderful wit, is now so deaf that conversation is limited to the absolute basics. Miriam.

★

There are times when we have a "Book of Job" chapter. This is when everything we touch seems to go wrong, when fate appears to conspire against us and we are sorely tested.

Whilst these temporary states of sadness and difficulty are part of being human, not expressing them, bottling them up, can lead to unnecessary stress and a sense of isolation.

It is not possible to be happy all the time; the intensity of happiness and joy is partly because it is fleeting. Acceptance and contentment, however, are more realistic and achievable goals, and something we can aim for in preference. Anything more ambitious is likely to result in loss.

★

I had an early menopause and when my periods finally stopped in my mid-forties I remember feeling I wasn't a complete woman any more. Even though I had two children and did not want any more, there was a discomfort in knowing I could not get pregnant. I was sure I was less "female" and convinced I would no longer be of interest to the opposite sex. It felt like the first nail in the coffin with regard to my ability to attract men. Caroline.

★

In addition to being a potential cause of depression, the menopause is a trigger for loss in some women who feel the lack of fertility reflects on their womanhood, and therefore on their identity. For these women there is a time of genuine grief which needs to be recognised. For others the end of menstruation and worries over pregnancy herald a new liberation.

The menopause is not called "the change" for nothing; it introduces a new stage in a woman's life but, as with all change, there is loss involved also.

However this biological process affects us, we need to acknowledge the emotions that arise and to take whatever steps we deem necessary to move on successfully to our new physicality. For some this will be a seamless transition to a greater maturity, whilst for others it could be another item destined for the loss box.

★

Increasing health challenges came home to roost for Michael when he went to the funeral of a friend of many years. The sad occasion reunited a group of people he was part of in his late twenties and early thirties, when many were settling down, getting married and having babies.

Here they were together again but in late midlife. Those who did not previously need glasses were now wearing them to read the service sheet, and there was more than one hearing aid visible from behind a conveniently arranged strand of hair.

★

When I was diagnosed with macular degeneration I had to make changes in my life that would help me cope with the gradual loss of my sight. The first thing to go was driving. It is several years now and I have adjusted more or less to using public transport, but it does mean I can't go on impulsive outings because everything has to be planned. It used to be that if the sun was shining I would hop into the car and go out to the countryside, or if I was feeling low I could ring a friend and suggest an outing somewhere. I am coping well generally, but along with the other things lack of clear eyesight brings, I do miss the freedom a car provided. Nancy.

★

Talk at the ensuing wake included the pros and cons of HRT (amongst the women), bad backs, hip or knee

102

replacements preventing effective games of golf, and methods of preventing or dealing with arthritis. Michael was in a state of shock for days afterwards, wondering where the years had gone and how they had arrived at this point in all their lives.

You will note that no one at the event above included sexual difficulties in their post-funeral chit chat. We can make jokes about sex until our hair turns pink, but being "real" about our bedroom antics, or lack of them, is a different matter altogether.

You can be absolutely sure that both loss of libido and impotence were there amongst the health issues in that (or any) group of people, and it seems such a pity that we are not able to be more candid about these problems which so many of us face at one time or another.

For some, sexual desire and virility remain until their dying day, but this is not a given and it certainly cannot be relied upon. Many a loss box content is associated with this area of our lives. Only by being open can men and women start to understand this area of potential loss from each other's point of view.

When Lucy was in her twenties she went out with an older man. Their romance was never consummated because he suffered from erectile dysfunction. Lucy had no clue what was going on because she was innocent of such things, but he explained that the more he cared about someone the more difficult it was for him to make it happen. She did not have enough confidence in herself to believe that or cope with the situation and took it as a reflection of her lack of sexual attractiveness.

Lucy felt inadequate and humiliated and so, no doubt, did her partner. Neither of them had an inkling of how each was feeling because a profound sense of failure on both sides blocked any sharing on the subject.

Now that she is more mature and aware of these matters it is obvious to Lucy that they needed to give one another much more reassurance. By not doing so, they damaged themselves and created needless loss of self-esteem.

Lucy walked away from that budding relationship not just because of the physical issues, but because the man in question was given to outbursts of bad temper. In retrospect she can see his behaviour may well have been frustration manifested in other ways. That does not make aggression acceptable but it does make it more understandable, and underlines further the necessity of good communication.

★

During my forties my virility started to wane. It has been a slow, gradual decline but it means I can no longer count on getting a hard on whenever I want to have sex. Men do not discuss sexual problems; they are a private matter. They are more likely to hide what they see as a sense of failure, even from their wives or lovers. For me it has been like carrying an injury; a pain that is isolating. I am horribly aware I am no longer in that state of readiness to perform and this loss of my manhood triggered a process of intense bereavement for my younger, more virile state. I realise how much my identity is tied up with sexual prowess; it is like something is broken. The possibility of not getting an erection causes me anxiety, and the fear can become a self-fulfilling prophecy. For me this is a particularly sensitive issue because my marriage did not work for reasons other than sex, so I am facing the possibility of humiliation not with someone who is an established long-term lover but with the prospect of a woman to whom I feel a need to prove myself. If that happens I hope I will have the courage to be open. I think honesty is the only way to take the pressure off, and being able to talk about it and to work through the problem with compassion might heal the hurt and the shame. In some ways this change of emphasis could be good because it requires the end of dependence on the physical to make a relationship work; there is less reliance on jumping into bed to connect. It could lead to a deeper understanding, a potentially richer source of love, and perhaps a degree of union I have not experienced before. Women should not underestimate the effect this decline in potency has on a man though; it is a grave sense of loss. Simon.

★

We are bombarded with sexual images everywhere, at every turn, with their tacit message that we should all be sexually active and competent. It would be easy to persuade ourselves that if sex is not top of our agenda, there must be something wrong with us.

The actuality is that there are those for whom sex is the be all and end all of life, those who can take it or leave it, those who would rather clean the windows or, God forbid, turn out the fridge, and all stages in between.

I cannot speak for the male of the species but from what I know of myself and other women close to me, our need for sex varies enormously. If my experience and that of my female friends is representative, however, women generally need less sex as they age.

I remember this drop-off in sex drive starting quite early, when there were babies and young children to care for. Luckily for me, and I suspect for most women, an interest in sex does return when parenting eases up, but never quite to the same level as it was pre-motherhood. For some this loss will take up considerable space in their loss box, and for others it will barely feature.

The physical and emotional demands of rearing a family mean there is little energy left for passion and gymnastics at the end of the day. I agree with whoever said conversation is the best foreplay, but when both parties are exhausted it is so tempting to flop in front of the television and zone out. Neither does talking over worries at work, nappy rash, baby feeding problems or who will deal with the bulging recycling bags count.

★

An elderly man once jokingly told me that if we put a coin in a jam jar for every time we had sex before marriage, and then transferred those same coins into a second jar on every occasion after tying the knot, the first jar would never be emptied.

This man was born in 1921, long before the permissive society was invented, so I was left wondering if he had had an untypically promiscuous youth, or an exceptionally deprived marriage. Either way, I cannot help feeling there is a degree of truth in his tale.

The spark that is present in a new or illicit sexual liaison is a thrill largely created by excitement of the unknown or potentially unavailable, and perhaps a frisson of danger or risk. The loss is that this heightened exhilaration cannot easily be maintained within a marriage, the very essence and value of which is familiarity, trust, steadiness, reliability and security.

During my years of caring for babies and toddlers, and from chatting with good friends at that time, I know most of us were happy to have sex, but preferably good sex now and again rather than more frequent "quickies". If we failed to initiate sex often enough to keep our husbands happy it was simply because, when every second of sleep was precious, we were no longer naturally inclined to do so.

I cannot see why things should have changed since my youth and these sentiments continue to be justified and reasonably predictable when young mothers are perhaps oozing breast milk, changing pooey nappies, clearing up sick, and churning out fish fingers and sausages by the dozen.

I needed to be reminded I was desirable all those years ago, and no doubt so do today's frazzled mums.

It should be said that the need to know they are still desired is also true for men, who not only often take a share in the parenting role in our modern society, but who can so easily feel displaced in their wife's affections when children come on the scene.

This is a time when it is all too easy for either party to be drawn to someone new who reminds them they are still attractive to the opposite sex, someone who can regenerate a fading sexuality and boost a flagging ego.

The loss box is beginning to bulge.

★

Whilst it is not an inevitability, the onset of midlife or old age can bring with it a gradually diminishing interest in, or ability to have, sex. This predicament is much more common than we care to admit.

My much loved but rather eccentric father was an exception to this conspiracy of silence, and in his later life he used to roar with laughter as he told anyone who cared to listen that it would require the expert skills of a snake charmer to persuade his recalcitrant nether regions to rise again to their former glory.

I also recall the reaction of my dry-witted mother when Viagra was invented. My father had died by that stage, so she was not necessarily referring to herself when she said she could hear a universal groan from older women in every corner of the planet who had previously heaved a sigh of relief that they did not have to bother with "that" any more.

Although there are no doubt exceptions, for post-menopausal women the changed levels of oestrogen, progesterone and testosterone naturally result in a reduced level of desire, and when you think about it this makes sense.

If sex is primarily for procreation and survival of the species, why would nature make women continue to feel a strong need for sex once this purpose has either been fulfilled or is no longer relevant? The fact that we now live for so many more years after this "change" is what requires us to look at how we deal with sexual matters in later life.

This is not to say older women are incapable of passion because, despite society's attitude, the young most definitely do not have the monopoly when it comes to love making. In particular, couples who meet and get together later in life sometimes report that sex has never been so good.

For those men not able to achieve an erection it does not necessarily follow that the desire and inclination is not still there, which can be a cause of great frustration, distress and loss.

I have also spoken to men who, despite the availability of various treatments for impotence, have happily laid their sex drive to rest, and will not be bothering the NHS on that score.

The complexity comes when partners have differing libidos or when one loses interest and the other is keen to maintain an active sex life. Where this exists one party can feel unwanted and rejected if there is no sex, and the other can feel used and exploited if there is.

★

I have retained my libido into my sixties and my sexual urges are still up and running, albeit slightly less than in my youth. Unfortunately the same cannot be said for my partner who has lost interest in what was once an important part of our relationship. I have had to look at the larger picture and remind myself of the things of value that remain, such as the fact that he makes me laugh every day, and focus on those. Penny.

★

Living alone, like so many others in today's society, I have been celibate for many years. Although I miss the intimacy of a loving sexual relationship, I try to convert this aloneness into something positive by consoling myself that I have read many more interesting and inspiring books whilst propped up on my pillows than I otherwise would have done. Sometimes I manage to convince myself, but not all the time. Much as I have a passion for literature, it is hard to beat the wonder and tenderness of being held in the arms of the person you love. In the end there is no fooling myself and I have to admit this remains a loss.

From those who are still in relationships in the autumn of their lives and are therefore more in the know than me, I am assured there really is life after regular, trouble-free sex. Where there is impotence, either occasional or permanent, there can still be love, cuddles and hugs.

Sex is not to be confused with intimacy; any one of us can have sex with a stranger but, by its nature, it is not intimate. Conversely we can have intimacy with the person we love without the sexual act.

Caressing and sensual touch without penetration as the ultimate outcome is sexual union of another kind. For some couples a change of dynamics takes place and a platonic relationship suffices, a loving companionship. There are no rules.

I love the story of the old couple who go for an annual check-up at their local health clinic. The husband, in his eighties, goes in first and tells the doctor he is worried because the first time he made love to his wife recently he was very cold afterwards, and the second time he was very hot and sweaty. When it is the wife's turn to go into the surgery, the much impressed GP tells her of her husband's concern that after intercourse the first time he was cold and after the second he was very hot. 'That might be' she replies, 'because the first was to celebrate New Year, and the second was in Greece, on our Summer holiday.'

If we are to avoid magnifying sexual problems we need a mature acceptance of each gender's vulnerability.

If I were to start a love affair now, in older age, I would be terrified of exposing my body after such a long time alone. My nakedness would not just be physical, with all its clearly visible signs of aging; I would be bearing my soul. Such a step would take enormous courage, but it is likely that my chosen partner would also have his doubts, fears and hang-ups. Not to take that risk if all else was right, however, would be a certain loss.

It is this depth of fragility and human frailty of which we need to be aware and which calls for compassion both for ourselves and our lover.

Mental, emotional and physical health can be affected by our loss of sexual potency or appetite, and each of us has to find our own way to accept this passing without being diminished. For some this will not be a problem, but for others it poses a challenge.

★

My mother was not a tactile person, and also being sent away to boarding school, I grew up craving the hugs I never got. As a result, I think, in adulthood I confused the physicality of sex with the sense of being loved that I had missed out on. When my long-term partner lost his libido it created a tremendous sense of loss because the importance of physical closeness had been sexualised into a need to be desired. I needed counselling to understand and come to terms with this loss. Emma.

★

There seems to be little room for what I refer to as the "Why me?" syndrome in respect to most things in life, and health is no different. When someone asks that rhetorical question I am always tempted to reply "Why not?".

Our bodies are such incredibly complicated structures that instead of wondering why so many things can and do, at times, go wrong with us, I am amazed that mostly it works so well.

We can and should do what we are able in order to stay fit but, to a large degree, health will always remain a lottery. Holding on to loss through health can surely only make our symptoms worse.

Happiness is nothing more than good health and a bad memory
Albert Schweitzer

EXERCISE 5

For as far back as my memory stretches I have suffered from digestive problems. That is, until two years ago when a friend sent me a cutting of a newspaper article about gluten intolerance. I decided to try eliminating gluten from my diet, and my life was transformed. I still have a more sensitive stomach than the average person, but the improvement has been life-changing.

When I was suffering particularly badly it was very tempting to be angry with my body for not working properly, but this negative emotion only made me feel worse.

What I decided to do in the end was to have occasional inner conversations with my intestines. Whilst I was lying in bed, driving, or washing-up I would use this time to tell my large bowel how difficult it was to enjoy life when I had gut ache, and how a bloated stomach made me look fat. I would offload my feelings about my condition and the distress it caused.

As this was a conversation rather than a monologue, I would then allow my innards a chance to give their point of view. I learned they were doing their best under very difficult circumstances, and that they felt under stress. There were suggestions about chewing more efficiently and not bolting my food. Why did I eat spicy foods when I knew they might upset me, and did I need to have more than one glass of wine? My poor stomach obviously felt its needs were being disregarded by me too.

This rather odd practice made me compassionate towards my body and its struggles, and encouraged me to work with it rather than seeing it as the enemy and the cause of my troubles. It was not the cure, but it stopped me feeling at war with my physical self, and lessened my resentment over the resulting loss of well-being.

One of the exercises we can do is to have a written conversation with whatever part of our body or mind is giving us trouble. We may just find we learn something new or are able to come to terms with the way things are. We could discover a level of sympathy for our physical selves which we had not previously known.

Just write "Dear Kidneys/spine/big toe", and take it from there. When you have got it out of your system write the reply.

Our bodies are doing their best.

CHAPTER SEVEN

Money and Success

The quiet mind is richer than a crown…
Such sweet content, such minds, such sleep, such bliss
Beggars enjoy when princes oft do miss
Robert Greene

Money matters are not as straightforward as we may think. To a degree, wealth can be subjective.

Amongst those I know, for example, I can bring to mind more than one person who thinks they are hard up and who worries almost constantly over their finances. In reality they live in large houses without mortgages, and although their concern over money means they are not profligate, they nevertheless maintain a comparatively high standard of living.

At the other end of the scale I know of others who scarcely have a penny to their name, who for one reason or another do not have pensions to look forward to, but who remain resolutely optimistic in their financial outlook.

The former may have an inbuilt fear of deprivation, and the latter may be dangerously in denial, but most of us are somewhere in between.

If you want to learn about attitudes to money, try collecting for charity in your street. If my experience was typical, it was sometimes in the poorer homes that I met with a smile and a willingness to give a donation. In these cases the coins amounted to very little but that was not the point; what they gave was what they had to give and they gave it freely.

It is second nature for some to hang on to every penny and

for others to have open palms and this approach to money is unrelated to our monetary status. Poverty can be a state of mind.

★

Zara's first marriage was to someone with little money and although they could pay their bills without too much trouble, luxuries like holidays, going out for meals, and outings generally were limited.

Some years after her husband died, Zara married a high earner, but someone who loved the good things in life. This meant that whilst they lived in a big house with a swimming pool and tennis court, had a boat, and went on ski-ing and summer holidays, she did not feel financially secure because the money went out as fast as it came in.

Zara and her husband also mixed with others who lived at this level, but who were earning enough to put substantial money aside as well. As a result the couple never considered themselves well off because their peers were usually wealthier.

The differential in her first and second husband's earning capacity failed to make Zara feel any richer despite her more opulent lifestyle.

★

Geoff and I had a large house, nice car, went on regular holidays and led a reasonably financially carefree life. In the late 1980s, Geoff started a business and the investment needed was set against our family home. When the recession of the early nineties hit the property market, on which our business was reliant, we believed the forecasts that it would be a short-lived dip and borrowed more and more money to stay afloat. When it came to a point where the company was no longer viable, we had no option other than to sell our much loved house to pay off the debts. When the crunch finally came, it was

almost a relief. Since then, and in addition to both of us working full-time,
Geoff and I have bought, lived in and sold numerous properties, doing them
up and moving on to increase our equity. We have now settled in a small
terraced house. Neither of us is denying that extra money would be welcome,
and we would both like our future to be more financially stable than it is, but
other than that we have most of what we want. There is no doubt that our
experience still takes up a large chunk of our individual loss boxes and needs
clearing out. Bea.

★

In this latest recession there are scores of people in financial
difficulty; those who have been made redundant in a market
where new jobs are scarce or at an age when it is difficult to
start again, and business owners who have been unable to ride
the storm.

There are those who have saved all their lives and now, in
retirement, find the interest rates bring them little to live on.
For others, pension plans have been shattered by the collapse
of large institutions or terms that have changed, and they may
have to find a way to go on working for many more years than
they intended.

There is little in life that cannot be taken from us; this is
true of friendship, health, work, and love. Wealth and financial
security are no different. As the recent market crash has
shown, no job, organisation or investment is one hundred per
cent reliable. If we define ourselves by money or possessions
we will undoubtedly experience a heightened sense of loss
should matters not go as we hoped.

★

Lack of financial security for whatever reason can be akin to
depression; it can take the shine off everything in life. The

drive to have a secure income and to know we and our family are safe is a fundamental human impulse, a motivator, and this assured stability is key to happiness for most people.

★

My financial position has been affected by my mental health. I must have a fragile mental make-up because when my girlfriend left me for my best friend in my twenties I had a breakdown. I put a barrier around my feelings, and have never allowed myself to care deeply for anyone since. I have suffered depression to one degree or another from that time, and this has affected my capacity to hold down a job. I came from a well-to-do family but I have very little money myself because of my mental instability and I have lost the standard of living that I was brought up in. I live alone and lead a restricted existence but I manage to stay largely self-supporting which is important for my self-respect. Rob.

★

Having been a full-time mother, wife and homemaker for nearly twenty years, Maggie did not have an established career to fall back on when she got divorced. She trained herself up to become computer literate and took a job in hospital administration, rising eventually to a minor managerial role. She now runs a moderately successful B&B. Neither has earned her much more than a living wage and there is no room for anything other than necessities. Maggie loves beautiful things and has a naturally acquisitive bent which she has been forced to curb.

For Adrian, losing almost all his money through an unwise investment has involved changing his inner circle of friends. However much he continued to like the people he had known in the past, it proved almost impossible to retain common ground because what he could afford to do and take part in was so different. In the years since his loss, Adrian has built up a new social life with people who are closer to sharing his financial circumstances.

Loss of financial security has an impact that stays in the psyche and for those of us who experience such happenings, it can dominate our loss box.

Ella had a thriving clothes design business with over a hundred outworkers with whom she had a personal and friendly relationship. She regularly showed her work at the Milan and New York fashion shows, and earned enough money to keep her family in a nice home, educate her children, drive a smart car and to live well.

Because design was her passion, Ella concentrated solely on the creative side of the company. When her business manager introduced a wealthy investor who wanted to help her expand, Ella agreed without thinking it through sufficiently, trusting in the advice she was given.

In no time, the work was transferred to the Far East for mass production and the orders accelerated from a steady, reliable flow through small upmarket outlets into multiples through department stores. Shipments failed to arrive on time, the standard of the product declined, and the business failed.

Ella now lives in a small farm cottage, drives a hand-me-down car, has a tenant to help pay her bills, and works in a mundane job where her talents are wasted. Aged over sixty, she does not feel in a position to pick and choose employment, and as she lost all her savings with the business, she must continue to work into old age.

What is so remarkable about Ella is that she has managed to let go of her loss. She is sad that she is not able to earn a living doing what she so loves, but she has not held on to what might have been.

Of all the people I have met in my life Ella encompasses

what it means to be free of resentments, regret and disappointment; she just gets on with what is. By rights, Ella's loss box should be full to bursting, but it seems the lid is permanently open, and no sooner does something land than it flies out again.

★

If we change our attitude to failure in any walk of life, we can learn to see it as a friend. It offers us an opportunity to learn and grow. If we succeed in an aim, we get what we had hoped for and that is a positive achievement. If things do not go according to plan and we fail to accomplish our original aim, however, it is possible that we will achieve more in other ways. Success can narrow our horizon, whereas failure may broaden our perspective and drive us to expand our ideas in unforeseen directions.

Trevor and Pat had their lives sorted. They knew exactly what they were going to do in retirement, how things would pan out in their future, and over the years they had put funds aside in readiness. Unfortunately, what they could not predict was that Pat would suffer a serious and life threatening injury in a car crash. All their plans fell apart at that point. As someone who was self-employed Trevor had been meticulous in covering the possibility of illness on his part, but not on his wife's account. After being discharged from several months in hospital, Pat needed a high level of care and for a while Trevor was not able to give his business the attention it required. Later, he spent the majority of their savings on carers so he could get back to work, rebuild his client base and save his company. Pat's mobility has improved with time, although it is unlikely she will recover completely. What this experience has done for Trevor, is to teach him that being together and

Pat's well-being is worth far more than anything they might have had planned in their minds. He speaks of how they have learned to appreciate what they have now rather than focusing on what might be at some future time. He has come to terms with the fact that they are unlikely to have the finances to live the way they imagined when he stops working, but is happy that at least they have each other.

In many ways those whose stories I have recounted have felt the same about their money troubles. They would not want to go through the experience again, and although they have dealt with the cause and still carry the scars, they have also learned so much and grown in strength of character because of what they went through. It seems they have each found their own way to minimise their loss.

*

Where we can sometimes go wrong in modern society is to associate material prosperity with success in a wider sense. There is no denying that those who have acquired wealth through their own efforts have achieved financial success. The problem comes when we see such status as the sole or primary indicator of accomplishment in our work lives, and that without this overt proof of our attainments we have somehow failed to make the grade.

For every man or woman who makes his or her fortune through hard work there are multiple thousands who apply themselves with equal vigour, and who may succeed in their field, but do not become rich as a result. It is by linking the idea of a successful career to monetary recognition that we can create a loss of self-worth, fulfilment and satisfaction.

*

When I first met my husband he was working in a creative role backstage in the world of theatre and I found him inspirational and exciting to be around. He was very dynamic and successful and we mixed with famous people and led quite a wild life. He wasn't paid mega bucks but he earned reasonable money and we had a good standard of living. Once we settled down with a family and were approaching our forties he seemed to lose his motivation and his creative spirit. I worked part-time teaching the violin, but as a result of this change in his personality it was necessary for me to become the main breadwinner working in a number of schools. He shows no sign of returning to his former self and although old friends give him the odd bit of freelance work, he does not contribute very much to the day-to-day costs of running a home. I have to give him his due as a house husband though, and he is brilliant at looking after the children whilst I am at work. Although we are still together, and are not unhappy, I feel to a large degree I have lost the man I married, and I have certainly lost the financial status and security we once had and which I had hoped for myself and my family. I had to let go of what I had expected both in my relationship and in material terms because it was getting in the way of my happiness. I still feel a sense of loss but it is okay. Delia

★

Those who have acquired vast riches are no more certain to hold the key to successful living and contentment than those on a more average income. Granted, they do not have a churning sensation in the gut when the bank statement drops through the letterbox, but that is as far as it goes. It may well be that in their striving for material success they have lost out in other ways.

Angie, a retired nurse, took a temporary job working for an ultra wealthy family based in London. At one stage the household was flown by private plane to a winter resort where Angie spent several months of her employment also in the company of an heiress, one of the richest and, at that time, most famous women in the world.

It is interesting to hear of the insecure, unpredictable and positively neurotic behaviour of some of these individuals, of their separation from the lives of ordinary citizens, and their apparent unhappiness.

Listening to Angie's candid account I am aware of how much these people had lost by becoming so rich that they were no longer part of a larger society. It appears they had lost touch with what was real.

There is many a tear behind even the smartest front door and whilst extreme wealth may protect us from a few of the more commonly experienced losses in life, paradoxically it can introduce others at which few would guess.

The American film star, Brad Pitt, has intimated that the attributes of beauty, wealth and fame are negative karmas which can stop us finding true happiness. As he has all of these in abundance, he should be in a position to know.

Loss permeates every strata of society and no one is immune, money or no money, success or no success.

*

In terms of inheritance, gain can also be loss in differing ways. Bruce is a young man whose financial position means he does not have to work if he does not wish to do so. The fly in the ointment for him comes from the source of his family money, which his grandfather made by manufacturing armaments.

Bruce is fiercely anti-war and idealistic in his belief that there should be no such thing as armies, even for defence purposes, and that no country should develop, manufacture, sell or own weapons. He is also trying to rid himself of the guilt of inheriting what he sees as dirty money by training in a career that will help society.

During our conversation I was tempted to suggest he gave his inheritance away to CND or Campaign Against the Arms

Trade, and that he started his life again without what for him was obviously a burden. It is clear his wealth has brought him only angst.

The story of Matthew is different but the outcome is still one of a legacy creating loss. Over centuries, Matthew's family had owned a large farm in the north of England, and a beautiful manor house set in glorious countryside. He was a young single man with a love of fast cars and a zest for life when both his parents died within months of each other, and he took on the estate.

Forty plus years later he lives alone in his vast house, the majority of which is shut off and scarcely used. Reduced profits from dairy and arable farming no longer allow him to employ a farm manager or many farm hands. His strong sense of custodial obligation, however, does not allow him to sell what has been handed down to him so he works from morning until night to keep the operation going.

In honouring this legacy so steadfastly, his freedom to live a more expansive life has been curtailed, and he has grown reclusive with time. Because he limited his life to running the estate at the expense of a social life, he has never married, and by narrowing his horizons to such a degree he lost sight of one crucial factor – he does not have a child to whom he can bequeath his beautifully preserved asset.

Hannah's family background was not wealthy, but in her forties she met and married a man who had amassed a fortune. They had only been married a few years when he developed a terminal illness and died very shortly after. The couple did not have children, so Hannah found herself with a great deal of money but very lonely. For her, the loss involved in being in her financial position was that she doubted people's intentions in being her friend, especially men who wanted to date her. She was unsure about their motivation and sincerity.

These illustrations are indicative of inherited wealth or assets being a double-edged sword and having the potential to create significant loss.

★

Another area worthy of consideration is the difference between being wealthy in material terms and being rich in the wider sense.

Joan is an octogenarian great-grandmother who cycles everywhere she can, using her battered old car only when necessary. She does voluntary work on Saturdays, helps children to read in a local school, sings in a choir, looks after her youngest grandchild regularly, writes poetry and short stories, cooks wonderful cakes, models for artists, loves to dance when the opportunity arises and reads the *Guardian* every day. She plays the cello with a group of local musicians and gives weekly lessons to a neighbour. She has an ever ready smile, a marvellous sense of humour, is a whizz at crosswords, and has always got a book she wants to talk about and pass on.

For her eightieth "do", Joan hired the village hall, and because she has very little money she asked everyone to contribute to the food. This meant the guests felt included and an integral part of the event.

There were people of all ages at the party, quite a few of whom had come some distance. There was poetry dedicated to her, and a hilarious song a friend had written and which was performed with accompanying backing and dance from her daughter and some of her grandchildren. Two of her granddaughters had rehearsed a rendition on their violins as a tribute. The love in the room was palpable, and if ever there was a successful life this was clearly it.

Joan has brought up five children, one of whom, a successful poet, died in her forties. She has worked as a paediatric nurse, run a playgroup, and been warden of a Quaker Meeting where she cared for numerous tenants, some of whom were students far from home who adopted her as a surrogate mother figure.

She now lives in a modest house, buys most of her clothes from charity shops and is one of the most contented people I know. She has no money to speak of but she is rich and her life is a success. This is invisible wealth.

With the above examples and comparison I am not insinuating that those with money are not also successful human beings. I am saying that despite what the value system of our culture would have us believe, wealth and successful living are not automatically synonymous. Neither, of course, are they mutually exclusive, but wealth in purely financial terms is only one part of a much larger picture.

★

I retired last year and subsequently moved into a much smaller house. Most of my furniture had been passed down through the family and was too large for my new home. I had to decide what I could keep, and in the end it transpired that very little would fit in and I would have to let go of the bulk of it. My children had enough furniture of their own and could not take much so I gave it to various people I cared about, and to charity. It was really painful saying goodbye to these familiar items which had been my stalwart companions for so many years and which held untold memories. I had to persuade myself it was a release to own very little and that I would feel lighter somehow. In the end I found I could be just as happy without so many material possessions and giving them away helped me to make a new start. Lisa.

★

Lots of pound notes in the bank does not, by itself, convert into meaningful living or a life that is rich, just as little money does not necessarily mean someone is not living an abundant or valuable existence. Having plenty of money is a wonderful position to be in; it is when we seek wealth purely for its own sake, rather than as a justly earned reward for our focus on other achievements, that we lose.

★

The super rich help to keep the economic wheels turning and by doing so they provide others with essential employment. They are also in a prime position to make the world a better place if they choose to do so.

At the time of writing, sixty-nine of the four hundred richest people in America have signed a Giving Pledge to donate the majority of their wealth to needy causes, the arts, sport and other philanthropic causes which improve the lives of others.

With the current recession and the ensuing cuts in government funding in the UK, the reliance of charities on the generosity of "super donors" who are able and willing to offer financial support is increasing.

With this admirable and healthy attitude to money everybody benefits; those donors who are self-made have had the achievement of becoming rich through their own graft and skill, and they gain the feel-good factor of passing a share of it on to others.

Bill and Melinda Gates, and no doubt many others who are less in the public eye, take this one step further by involving themselves practically with the work of the charities they support. This is philanthropy in capital letters.

For those who have inherited their wealth and also decide to give a portion of it away, no doubt the sense of making a difference to society is equally satisfying. There is little we do for others that does not help the giver as much as the receiver; we lose to gain, and in this way money and success combine.

★

The intention of advertising can be to hoodwink us into believing our social status, identity and happiness come from consumption. Research has shown, however, that money and happiness go hand in hand only so far.

★

My husband was a high-flyer who earned a lot of money and we had a beautiful home, but I was in a loveless marriage. I tried very hard to make things work but in the end I had to make a decision whether or not to leave. A number of those in my social circle were not happy in their marriages either but they stuck it out because they liked their lifestyle and the financial benefits of being married. I was not comfortable with this arrangement and I was aware that the mistake in marrying was just as much mine as it was my husband's and, although I did not love him, I had to acknowledge he was a good man. Because of this I knew that if I left him I did not want to take more of his hard-earned money than I absolutely needed in order to survive. In the end I did decide to leave him, and although I had little in the way of qualifications I have worked hard at a series of jobs to earn my own way as much as possible ever since. My present life is unrecognisable from the way I once lived, but I am being truer to myself. I have lost a great deal in material terms but I have found a new peace. Zoe.

★

As has already been mentioned, money is vital to happiness in terms of security and paying the day-to-day living bills, and it continues to have a substantial influence on our emotional well-being to the point when we have an adequate home, a reliable car to ferry the family around, and a holiday each year. From that point on the link weakens.

This has been borne out amongst people I have known.

Almost without exception the most contented are those who have adopted a non-consumerist lifestyle regardless of their position in terms of money; they have enough to pay their overheads without worry but do not hanker for more and more material possessions. They have learned the meaning of "enough", and they have not succumbed to what the clinical psychologist and author, Oliver James, writes of so aptly as "affluenza". It is in affluenza that we can so easily lose our way and ourselves.

Jerome K Jerome sums this up when he writes: "Let your boat of life be light, packed only with what you need – a homely home and simple pleasures, one or two friends worth the name, someone to love and to love you, a cat, a dog, enough to eat and enough to wear."

If we adopt this healthy attitude to money and success our loss box will be less burdened.

To be content with what we possess
is the greatest and most secure of riches
Marcus Tullius Cicero

EXERCISE 6

I particularly enjoy this exercise because it makes me so grateful for what I have.

Draw a number of large stars on a sheet of paper. As with the gingerbread men exercise for a previous chapter, I use star biscuit cutters in my workshops, or let people use freehand drawn stars if they prefer. I know we can download stars from the internet but creating the page ourselves is part of the process. As the essence of this book is about accepting imperfection in ourselves, others and our lives, it is helpful not to struggle to get the star shapes just so.

Give this page a title such as Friendships, Riches, Successes, Interests, Hobbies, Love, Family.

As an example let us imagine we have chosen the title of Friendship. In this instance we can fill each star with the name of a friend and then put in descriptive words of what this person provides in our life, such as loyalty, reliability, sensitivity, generosity, support, shared history. We might then put in emotions which are evoked on our part such as appreciation, admiration, kindness, warmth. We can include memories such as "Greece" to represent a holiday we spent together.

As another example, on a page entitled Riches we can fill each star with good things in our lives that money cannot buy. Depending on our circumstances these may include family, good friends, humour, beautiful countryside, fitness, agility, music, flowers, sport, good looks, our eyesight, faith, talents and abilities, a satisfying job, a view from our window or the sense of belonging provided by our local community. Alongside these we can put the emotions which result from these riches.

If I was to do a star page of success for myself right now, I would include getting this far with writing *The Loss Box*. As I sit at the computer I have no idea if it will be published or if anyone will read it. Whatever the outcome, however, I have almost completed what I set out to do. That, in itself, is a success. So is managing to get some Christmas presents at half price in the sale. So is teaching my Jack Russell to stop and wait when I want to put her on the lead. So is making mayonnaise without it curdling. Our lives are full of small successes if only we take time to recognise them.

Some years ago I adopted a Buddhist practice of developing gratitude. I have a notebook at the side of my bed, and before turning out my light at night I try to remember to write a list of things to be grateful for in the day which has passed. I sometimes find myself reluctant to pick up the book because I believe the day has not been particularly good or fruitful. Once I start writing, however, I often find I can fill a page or more. The items are usually small, such as birdsong, seeing a robin in the garden, the joy of a good book to read, or the luxury of sitting up in bed with the comfort of my hot water bottle in the hollow of my back on a freezing cold night. It may be sunshine on a dog walk, one of my grandchildren laughing, a delicious bowl of pasta, a telephone call from a friend, making an arrangement to go to the cinema. This practice helps me to fall asleep in a positive and grateful frame of mind.

There may be losses connected to this chapter, but most of us are richer and more successful than we know.

CHAPTER EIGHT

Growing Older

Age is an issue of mind over matter. If you don't mind, it doesn't matter.
Mark Twain

For those of us who are lucky enough to make it into older age, there is a moment when we hear a creaking sound as the scales of mortality tip and there is considerably more weight on the past than on the future.

In truth this may have happened some years before but, like a supersonic jet, it takes time for us to hear the *boooooom*.

How well I remember my frugal mother buying a cashmere coat and justifying the expense by telling us it would "see her out". She was in her sixties, my age now and, true to her word, she was still wearing that coat up until her death at eighty-six.

Lately I find myself saying the same sort of thing to my own offspring about so much that I buy, whether it is a car or a washing machine, and from discussions with peers, they are doing likewise.

What this means is that we have lost our youthful air of invincibility and immortality. There is an amusing Italian saying which goes "Everybody will die. Perhaps I will too." We become aware that if everything on this earth is transitory, that must, by default, include us.

★

When we reached our sixties, Hetty and I downsized to a smaller house. Both of us were physically and mentally fit but, because we had no intention of moving again, we had the future in mind. The new home had to be in walking distance of the shops and a bus stop, and within easy reach of a station. The staircase had to be straight should either of us need a stairlift in our dotage, there must be a downstairs loo, and the garden should be small enough to be manageable. Neither of us could bear the idea of being a burden to our children so this was serious forward planning and, in our minds, a practical and pragmatic way to avoid loss of independence. Neil.

★

Facing up to a stage of winding down and our eventual and unavoidable demise can be a catalyst for another period of reflection. It can bring with it the welcome clarity of what is important. With such musing, however, can also come disillusion, lamentation for paths not taken, and more soul-searching over aspirations not realised, hopes not fulfilled. Perhaps we had an unformulated, vague idea that we would have made a difference, but this has not come to fruition in any recognisable fashion.

What haunts so many of us as we grow older is the not knowing what might have been. We may be inclined to see those things that did not work out, and things we lost rather than those we gained.

This is the stage when we need to come to terms with our lives. In our darker moments of casting our minds back we can misinterpret our past as a catalogue of errors or wrong turns. How easy it is to have an "if only I had known" regret. The fact is we did not know, and very often it is only by making a decision in ignorance that we learn. Apart from the odd downright foolish moment, it is likely that we will have lived almost entirely doing what seemed right at the time. Granted, it may not always seem a good choice now but how wonderful is the power of hindsight, and how worthy we are of our own compassion and self-forgiveness.

I am a member of a relaxed and happy all-age a cappella singing group – a choir would be a misnomer – who meet weekly. Our abilities range through excellent, quite good, mediocre, right down to pretty dire. I represent the latter category. We sing purely for the pleasure of it, and occasionally perform in the street or a local pub for an unsuspecting public. Our inspirational and energetic young leader tells us not to fear making a mistake or going wrong. If we go off tune or forget the words we have merely added interest and individuality to our performance, and spiced up the sound. "Sing out" she commands, "give it all you've got. Feel the joy and don't get too hung up on getting it right."

I think this is a great analogy for life and perhaps it is how we might deal with what we could otherwise have considered our past errors and wrong turns. They might just have added interest, spice and individuality and we can let them go just as we might with the future blips which are no doubt waiting to happen. So what if we did not, or do not, get it all right? It is surely better to feel the joy and give life all we have got, in whatever way that is for each of us.

We need to appreciate our tenacity and strength, and ponder with awe at how we survived the blows and the struggles with which we were undoubtedly faced.

The twentieth century medical pioneer, Dr Elisabeth Kübler–Ross, dedicated a large part of her life to working with the dying, and as a result she became an expert on grief. She wrote of the most "beautiful" people being those who had known suffering and loss, and who had found their way out of these depths. In her experience "beautiful" people did not just happen, they were the product of knowing loss, suffering and defeat and finding a way to overcome it. I believe this applies not only to bereavement and trauma, but to loss in general.

★

Recognising that I can no longer play golf as well as I once could, and that my son is better than I am at the game, has been a hard loss to swallow. This may sound unimportant but my pride took a blow I was not prepared for and it knocked me sideways. Until then, I was in denial about growing old. Matt.

★

When we are young we tend to look straight ahead, in middle age we may look both forward and back, but as an older person we are inclined to look only behind.

This truism has an obvious root; why would anyone facing old age and departure from this world choose to look too far to the future? The problem is that although looking back can be a source of heartwarming reminiscences, it can also be painful. It can set in motion a longing for a life that no longer is, for people who no longer are, and for a lost younger self.

It may be we have put things off for a special "someday" in the future. We might have intended starting a business, taking up painting, writing a book, learning golf or just allowing ourselves to be happy when that "someday" came along. One of the common shocks, however, of older age is the loss of possibilities. If we recognise our future is limited, so surely are the opportunities to fulfil our dreams. Did we miss that "someday", or is it now?

★

One of the most significant losses to my mind is the loss of a future, which happens when you get older. I have always found comfort in the idea that it was okay to plod on through whatever I was dealing with at any stage of life because true happiness and fulfilment was somewhere ahead of me, in some sort of nebulous future happening – I am not sure what. There is so much I

134

still want to do, so I had better stop plodding, and get on with it whilst I still can. Delia.

★

If we have not done so before, this might be the time to take up the discipline of what Buddhists call "living mindfully". By staying in the present we are not so prone to being taken up with regrets for things past or yearning for our lost youth, and neither are we taken hostage by apprehension of what might be to come.

This is not an easy practice as a permanent state of being, but once we are aware of the principle we can gradually incorporate it into our lives as a helpful tool to achieve contentment.

★

For me this later period of reflection, or older-life crisis, started in my fifties and gathered pace until it broke into a full pelt gallop around my sixtieth birthday.

Just as with the period of self-assessment in early middle age, or whenever it strikes us, this offers a wonderful opportunity to let go of the contents of our loss box, congratulate ourselves on getting to where we have got, and to take a fresh look at what brings us joy and happiness, whether it is reaching for new goals, devoting time to a hobby, or doing very little.

I am not suggesting this process is necessarily easy and I would not want to underplay the discomfort that it may involve. I have found facing myself and my life at this time excruciatingly painful in parts, but I believe it will pay dividends in the years I have left.

Yet again, we need to adopt an attitude of forgiveness for ourselves, others and life. We may not have done things perfectly, people may not have treated us well or as we would have liked, life may not have turned out as we had imagined, but that does not necessarily mean it has gone wrong, been faulty, or lesser than it should have been.

I am now in a position to say in all honesty that this is the best that my life has been, and I know many others of a similar age who feel the same.

★

A well documented fact of aging is that we are no longer seen. Like most women, Janice was lucky enough to get her fair share of male attention and admiration in her youth not, she insists, because she was especially good-looking but merely because she was young. Walking down the street nowadays and in her late fifties she goes almost entirely unnoticed, not only by the opposite sex but by people in general, and more than once she has been bumped into by young people who simply have not noticed her.

Janice admits that, just as it does not rain upwards, gravity is winning where her body is concerned and all is a little on the droop. Nevertheless, she has not become overweight, she does not wear frumpy clothes, and she still takes trouble over her appearance and is stylish. She has simply grown older.

★

I remember a trip to London with my fourteen-year-old daughter, Megan, and noticing how men were looking at her more than at me. I was only thirty-seven at the time and still looking reasonably good, but I now know it was the start of an all encompassing and ongoing process where we hand over our roles to the next generation. Many years later, and after a fairly bumpy period of mourning, I can say this is a passing I am now willing to take out of my loss box. I can give thanks for the compliments I received in my younger days, and I am finally able to kiss this attention goodbye with a fairly happy heart. Sophie.

★

This gradual loss of sexual attractiveness and, indeed, general presence is mildly unnerving at first and could understandably result in a sense of grief. Alternatively, once we have become adjusted to being more or less overlooked in physical terms, it can be a welcome liberation from the shallow demands of the ego and an opportunity to focus our attention elsewhere.

I am conscious it is a cliché, but in my own experience it is true to say I am more aware of birdsong, of trees in bud, of the funny noise a frog makes when he is trying to attract a mate, of the innocence of a small child skipping down the street, of a kind smile, of the wagging tail of a happy dog, or of the multiple small wonders of the world going on around us.

Snatching a break from writing this chapter, I took my dogs for a walk in the woods and watched a red winter sun setting behind a line of trees on the distant hills. I was struck not only by the beauty itself but by the deep appreciation I felt at seeing this spectacle of nature, something I might never even have noticed or given a second glance in my callow youth. We may wave goodbye to much as we age, but other joys come in their stead.

That I am not the only one to come to this conclusion is obvious to a reader of Germaine Greer's book, *The Change*. She admits that when she arrived in East Anglia in the mid-sixties, aged twenty-five, she did not notice the huge skies of that open landscape. Evidently she was too preoccupied with inventing herself to find time to stop and stare, to value her natural surroundings. She writes of walking the same paths now but without the distraction of her ego or seeking attention for herself. Instead, she wants to see and absorb what is going on around her and to be open to the experience of the moment.

Many of us will relate to the growing pleasure to be found in nature, heightened awareness and in observation generally. There is no denying, however, that growing older also involves an ever increasing experience of loss, and we have to come to terms with an altered reality.

★

Needing glasses is a pain as you age. I not only resent the loss of eyesight which meant I could read the ingredients on a jar or cooking instructions without holding my arm extended, but also the loss of memory which, when I acknowledge I need my glasses, sends me round the house on a wild goose chase wondering where the hell they are. Margaret.

★

My sister once gave me some words of simple wisdom which I have found helpful over the years. If I notice yet more wrinkles or I momentarily despair at the sight of my aging reflection in the mirror, I remember her advice to relish how we are at that moment, because in five years time we would give anything to look as we do today.

Compassion for our physical state can also help with accepting the aging process. I can look at my body and thank it for all it has endured over my lifetime. It has been a trooper and, despite the fact that I have not always treated it with the respect it deserves, it has done its very best for me.

★

The past is what made us who we are, but we can choose what parts of it we take into our future. By letting go of our losses, hurts and misgivings we do not leave them behind as though they have been of no consequence, we just decide not to allow them to have power over us, affect us negatively or control us. We can learn the lessons they taught us and move on.

If we choose it, this can be a time of resurrection, of re-invention; we have the option to start again at any age.

★

I spent the first half of my life in a state of "incuriosity" about life. I am not sure what awakened me from my mental slumber, but I am so mad that I wasted so many years and cannot bear to think of the loss of all I could have done, seen and experienced. Tessa.

★

One of the ways I reacted to this later reassessment was to write a personal "yet to do" list, which I am steadily working my way through and which helps me to concentrate more on the here and now and on the near future, rather than on the past.

I pictured myself revving gently at the starting gate of the last few laps. What could I achieve that was worthwhile; what could I do that would provide new satisfaction; where have I always longed to travel; what am I capable of giving back to society before I run out of fuel or my engine stalls?

★

There is little doubt we will wave goodbye to our dependent children, our careers, youth, firm flesh, supple limbs, good eyesight, sharpness of memory – so many goodbyes – and yet it is imperative that we do not put these in our loss box. Instead, as they depart, we can say hello to the many new delights on offer.

We are still who we are and we are of value. We have acquired so much wisdom on our journey to this point. It may be that no one wants to hear us spouting what we have learned, but there are other ways to impart wisdom. We can live it.

The young are responsible for most of the innovation and exciting new ideas and that is how it always has been and should be, but we oldies hold the balance. By living our wisdom with a good grace and plenty of humour we can bring necessary experience, caution, and ethical and moral values into the equation, some of which we have learned the hard way.

We are an essential cog in the wheel of life, and a few grey hairs do not mean we are on the scrapheap. It is true that we make different contributions to society at different stages of life and at different ages. Growing older is just one more stage.

★

I lost my memory somewhere along the line, together with the sharpness of my mind. They probably migrated to the same place as my energy, which decided to do a bunk when it heard the words "sixty-five" and which requires me to sit down as soon as the six o'clock news comes on, and preferably not move again all evening. People's names, book and film titles, the whereabouts of car keys are daily challenges. After just one glass of wine it takes contributions from the fading memory bank of several equally dotty friends just to complete one comprehensive sentence, let alone a whole conversation. There are undoubtedly good sides to growing older but diminishing brain cells is not one of them. Julie.

★

A need to slow down is natural as we age, but with luck we can supplant physical busyness and striving with previously untapped interests. One of the riches I have discovered in my latter years is the art of lifelong learning and I am frustrated that there are not enough hours in the day to do all the courses and workshops on offer.

At art exhibitions, visits to open gardens and stately homes I am always impressed by the number of seriously elderly people looking at the art works, plants, or furnishings with genuine interest. What a priceless gift is curiosity, the enquiring mind; these people have maintained a passionate engagement with life.

On his deathbed in 1691, George Fox, founder of the Quaker movement, is recorded as having said the simple words "I'm glad I was here". I believe that this short sentence has the power to guide our lives. If our attitude can be one of "it's alright", one of turning loss into letting go and moving on, we are more likely to find the harmony and contentment we seek. We can incorporate our disappointments, failures and regrets into the rich pattern of our lives and set our hearts not to dwell on what did not materialise but to find the joys in what did, and what is good in the "now".

We can acknowledge both what we have lost and what we have gained. We can not only be glad to be here, as in here in this world, but "here" where life has brought us.

It is my hope that by working on our losses and endings, and by recognising our continuing and vital role in society, we can be free to appreciate what was, what is and the riches we have, and not waste those precious years still remaining.

Be ready bravely and without remorse
To find new light that old ties cannot give.

Hermann Hesse

EXERCISE 7

Some years ago I qualified as a masseuse. I never felt inclined to use the qualification professionally, but for a while I used to call in to a local hospice on my way home from work on a Friday night. There I would massage the feet and hands of those patients who agreed to this gentle touch.

All of the patients were terminally ill and as they chatted to me it seemed they were trying to make sense of their lives. I was struck by the importance of this process.

My son has suggested that I write the story of my life for him and for future generations of our family, and I know one or two older friends who have already done this to great effect. I have made a start and will doubtless enjoy the challenge of adding chapters over the years to come.

One of the joys of this undertaking is the gradual unfolding of memories, and appreciation of the social history our stories reveal. I find myself making notes as snippets come into my mind.

Before the days of ubiquitous central heating, there is the memory of beautifully patterned frost on the inside of the bedroom window on winter mornings, liberty bodices, and plucking up courage to pick up the ice cold spoon to eat my porridge at breakfast.

I can conjure up the smell of tomatoes in the greenhouse. We would be sent to pick the ripe ones to have on toast after school in the summer. In winter there was the welcome sight of bread and dripping on the plate, something which would come with a health warning nowadays.

One of my jobs was to slow bake stale bread to break up

for dog meal, which would be mixed with the fresh meat scraps from the butcher which my mother would have laboriously diced into small cubes. There was no such thing as tinned dog food or ready-made dog mixer-biscuit as far as I was aware.

Whether or not anyone else is likely to see our offerings, we could still attempt an autobiographical account of our lives. We might find they have been more interesting than we thought, even if only to us.

If writing is not your thing, there is no need to be put off putting pen to paper. I recently heard of someone who had a book in which she wrote random memories as and when they appeared, one recollection often triggering another. These gems were not in sequence and there was no pressure to create a literary piece, but it was of great interest to those who loved her.

Our tales might include losses by the dozen, but there are likely to be many, many more delights to recollect and chronicle.

Everyone has a story. What is yours?

CHAPTER NINE

Conclusion

The wound is the place where the light enters you.
Rumi

Whilst *The Loss Box* was formulating in my mind I signed up for a day workshop on loss. As expected, this centred mostly on dealing with grief following a death, but discussions also included the types of losses we have seen here.

Amongst the thought-provoking comments was one introduced by the facilitator, which I have since found very helpful. This lady suggested we can "grow around" our losses. This is what I mean when I say we carry them with us but leave the pain behind. By "growing around" them we are accommodating them in our emotional history but releasing the sorrow.

As mentioned in the chapter on health, I have had a metal plate put into my ankle following a fall. It hurt quite a bit at the beginning but before I was discharged from outpatient care, the final x-rays showed clearly that the new bone tissue had accommodated the plate and screws.

I am still walking around with that metal plate and always will be; it has been incorporated into my body. I have "grown around" it, but although it niggles a bit from time to time, I do not let it worry me. I have no doubt we can do the same with our losses.

In one of the case studies included in this book, the contributor used the word "wistful". Although it is a gentle, non-aggressive sentiment, it has a power and emotional punch beyond its weight. Just saying this word can make me feel slightly sad.

The dictionary definition of "wistful" reads as "having or showing a feeling of vague or regretful longing". Much of what we have covered in the previous chapters could be described in these terms. I hope that we have touched on some ways to alleviate our moments of being wistful for what we have lost.

The exercises in this book are a demonstration of how I, personally, have dealt with my ragtag collection of losses. They are not a formula to be followed precisely or a guaranteed resolution. Depending on how major the loss is, we need to allow time for the act of each "letting go" to permeate our subconscious. This is not a process which should be hurried and there is no pressure to leap forward to deal with the next one on the list until we feel comfortable to do so and are confident the previous loss has been resolved.

What I am trying to achieve stems loosely from Gestalt psychology, gestalt being a German word for shape or form. If we can visualise each loss experience as a square in which only three sides have been pencilled in, it is by acknowledging and processing the loss that the final line can be drawn and wholeness can take place. An incomplete shape, therefore, is unfinished business.

The suggested exercises are possible ways of filling in that missing fourth side to the square, and demonstrations of how we can use ritual to do so. If they do not speak to you there is no reason why you cannot think of others that would. Whatever we decide to do I hope we can inject some laughter and fun where the opportunity presents itself and where it is appropriate.

These processes can be done alone or in the company of others who are attempting to do the same remedial work. For me, there has always been strength in sharing.

It may well transpire that we do not need any of the exercises contained here, or elsewhere for that matter, and that just knowing we are not alone in our sense of loss is enough to lift any burden we have been carrying.

Appreciating that our losses are more or less what are meant to happen – inevitable – might be sufficient to let go of the underlying pain we have held. If we take on board the fact that loss is just part of living, and that had we not met with this or that particular loss we could equally have had another in its place, we might have found the remedy we are seeking.

I feel it is important to stress again that however much someone you know may tell you they have not suffered loss, this is not how it really is. They may be telling you *their* truth, but it is not *the* truth. It is impossible to have a life that is not punctuated with loss. There will be those who have lived sheltered lives, barely straying far from their comfort zone, who have experienced less obvious loss than others but they cannot cheat life to the extent of sidestepping loss altogether.

It could be argued that limiting ourselves to an unadventurous existence, a little-used life devoid of challenge, is the most extreme form of loss.

If we do not love, we do not take the risk of intimacy. If we do not invest in deep friendships we are not acquainted with the level of vulnerability demanded. If we do not challenge our abilities we may never have to face failure. If we do none of these, we neither extend ourselves nor do we reap the rich rewards on offer.

Which is the greater loss: living life outrageously and to the full and facing the possibility of pain, or staying safe to the point of sterility and knowing very little of anything? Luckily, most of us find a compromise between these two extremes, so let us pat ourselves on the back for having the courage to stick our heads above the parapet. Life may have shot at us, and we may have been wounded on occasions but, more importantly, we have widened our horizons.

Loss is a natural and unavoidable consequence of a rich existence. It is the potential cost of hope, optimism and courage. A life without hope, optimism and courage is scarcely a life. Ergo loss is meant to be.

I will end with the uncompromising words of the Buddhist teacher Thich Nhat Hanh: "I am of the nature to grow old. There is no way to escape growing old. I am of the nature to have ill-health. There is no way to escape having ill-health. I am of the nature to die. There is no way to escape death. All that is dear to me and everyone I love are of the nature to change."

On the face of it these words, which are really about loss in various forms, could be seen as negative if not downright miserable. On further examination they offer us release. They tell us these facts, or losses, are simply part and parcel of being human and of the cycle of life, and they need our acceptance in order not to have control over us. Let us face them and then we can let them go and get on with living.

It would be facile to suggest this is a book of answers or certainties; as such I cannot say categorically what works for me will be appropriate for you. My hope is for each one of us to discover our own way to relinquish regrets and of approaching loss without losing.

Start with forgiveness and acceptance and you will not go wrong.

AND MORE …

It was not possible to insert into the chapters all the case studies I had garnered for this book. As each and every contribution has a value, I am including the following as an additional chapter for their own sake. The fact that they are not in the main body of *The Loss Box* is no reflection of their worth, and they do not appear in any particular order.

★

In the days when university tuition was free I was offered a place to study at Oxford, but my parents could not afford to contribute to my keep. As a result I went to university locally so I could continue to live at home. I have always felt slightly cheated of this opportunity and wonder if I lost out by not being able to take up the offer. After years of resentment, I have learned to stop myself imagining how much better my life would have been if I could have taken up that place because I will never know if that is true, so it is a pointless exercise. Hermione.

★

I was on a train which had some engineering problems and it was stuck for some considerable time on the track. Everyone around me was ringing or texting their nearest and dearest to warn them there was a delay and not to worry. All of a sudden it was like a smack in the face to me that, although I have lots of mates and a good social life, it made no difference to anyone that I would be late that night – there was no-one waiting for me. Despite being a strong and balanced character, I felt completely lost, as though I did not exist. For some reason I do not understand, I am still carrying this sensation of loss with me. Terry.

★

I have lost a sense of belonging. I cannot keep up with technology and what people talk about, including my children and grandchildren. I am reasonably computer literate and I use the Internet and email, but all this stuff about podcasts, downloading music on to your "I" this or "I" that, Twitter and Facebook is beyond both my understanding and my interest. I am not that old, not old-old as in ancient, but I feel apart from the modern world when it comes to this sort of thing. Jacks.

★

The end of Sunday shop closure was a personal sadness to me. I loved those weekends when no one was distracted into shopping and when we shared the cooking of a meal and, as a family, we went for a long walk before coming back to collapse with the papers in front of the fire. Maybe I am idealising the past and the happiness of these gatherings, but I feel the loss of those days set aside from commercialisation. James.

★

I have never considered myself vain, but now and again I catch sight of myself in a shop window or a mirror and think "Who is that old woman?" It almost takes my breath away when I realise it is me. Why didn't I appreciate my body and my taut skin when I had it? Losing one's youthful looks is hard. Barbara.

★

When my elderly parents died, I felt I had lost more than a mother and father. Even though I was middle-aged, married and with a family of my own, I felt orphaned. In a way I had lost who I was, the knowledge of being someone's child. It was weird and for a while I was completely disorientated. Richard.

★

I was brought up in South Africa and married an Englishman who had settled there. When apartheid was at its height we left, fearing a bloodbath, and settled in the UK. I am not racist in any shape or form, but my accent created hostility in England because people made judgements through prejudice. I left my family, friends and history behind but did not feel readily accepted here. I gradually lost my confidence. I love England now and my husband and I have a good life in a beautiful part of the country, but my confidence has never completely returned. Victoria.

★

Since my husband retired I miss listening to Radio 4. Doing the ironing, working in the kitchen or whatever I was doing, I used to immerse myself in really interesting programmes. I especially loved the afternoon plays, but nowadays he will walk into the room and want to chat in the middle of something I am listening to, so sometimes I don't bother to turn the radio on because I would just get frustrated. I know I am lucky to have a lovely husband who wants to discuss things with me and I don't feel I want to hush him. I am also aware that I do similarly annoying things to him at times. Nevertheless it means I have lost a bit of my routine which gave me great pleasure. Martha.

★

My partner and I moved out of town into a small, very picturesque village. At first it was fine and I loved being surrounded by countryside. After a while, however, I realised that although the people around us were extremely pleasant and welcoming, they were not "my tribe". I felt as though I was losing my sense of who I was. It was almost as though I was disappearing. After a couple of years, we sold up and moved back to town. Bella.

★

The loss of teeth has been surprisingly upsetting, the awful recognition that a part of one's body is lost and gone forever. I have had several molar implants and they look just like the originals so no one else could tell, but I know of course, and I acknowledge that this is an over-reaction to a relatively minor happening. Peta.

★

I would have liked my brother and I to have a close relationship in adulthood, especially since our parents have died, but we are so different and our lives have gone in such opposite ways that it has proved difficult to maintain the connection. We see each other a couple of times a year but he is not someone I feel I could turn to if I was in trouble, and if we were not related I don't think we would be part of each other's life at all. I have accepted things the way they are but I carry a sense of loss with me. Gina.

★

I was brought up with the family sitting round the table every Sunday for a roast. I kept this custom going with my children and insisted that, even as teenagers, it was the one time in the week they were expected to be at home together. Now they have grown up and have their own families I really feel the loss of these special times when we all had a chance to catch up on each others' lives over a shared meal. Mandy.

★

I had nice legs when I was young, but now they are covered in broken veins. Does this count as a loss? Janice.

★

Whilst having a short break from home I found myself close to where my parents lived for the last twenty years of their lives. I stopped the car on the edge of common land where we often used to walk with the family dogs. I had not been there for a few years so I was taken aback to find that the land immediately surrounding this quiet rural spot had been developed in an extremely unsympathetic fashion, causing the whole atmosphere of the place to change. I know it is irrational but I had a protective, almost territorial reaction because it was where I had known so many happy times. It was akin to someone violating a precious memory, as if they had opened up my photo album and defiled pictures from my past. As a species, we humans can be stubbornly resistant to change in principle as we grow older, but perhaps we are also allowed times when we feel a genuine, understandable and natural grief for how some things in our lives once were and are no more. Liz.

★

I have always loved shopping. I got so much pleasure from browsing in antique and bric-a-brac shops looking for lovely bits for the home, and I enjoyed clothes shopping too. I am amazed to find that I have lost that "desire to acquire" in later life. First of all we moved into a smaller house when the children left home, so it was a matter of getting rid of possessions rather than adding to them. After that the need for new and exciting things to wear seemed to pall. I just don't need new stuff anymore and I walk past shops with indifference when they would once have tempted me. Obviously this is wonderful for the bank balance, but it has left a hole in my life, and a sense of loss. Carol.

★

When I think of loss I am reminded of throwing out my television and of watching my old car being driven away. The television had served me well for nearly twenty years and the car was the first major thing I had bought and paid for by myself after my husband had left. Both the TV and the car held memories of rebuilding my life alone with my son, of quiet evenings watching programmes we both enjoyed and trips and holidays in the car that I was so proud of. My son has grown up now, and I have established an independent life, but both these objects were representative of what we had been through as a unit and, symbolically, I felt their loss quite deeply. *Hannah.*

★

There is so much I wish I had asked my parents before they died. I want to know about the history of the antique furniture and other items I have inherited and which I have known all my life and taken for granted. I want to know more about their upbringing and youth so I can understand what made them who they were. I just didn't think about it until it was too late so I am left with a feeling of loss. *Harry.*

★

As a single mother, when my children married and had families of their own I missed being central in anyone's life. It is right that their partners and their children should take that place and I do not resent it, but it does not mean that it is not a loss that I am no longer that special person to somebody. I have some really lovely friends who I know care for me very much, but I am not pivotal in their life and nor would I expect to be. Now my parenting persona is no more, I struggle to maintain a sense of who I am. Married people have their identity reinforced in a loving relationship, but those of us who live alone have no one to mirror us. *Ginny.*

★

The bond between an animal and its owner is especially strong when the owner lives alone. When I developed ME I was too weak to be able to care for my dog anymore and I had to find a new home for him. This nearly broke my heart at an already difficult time. I expect he adjusted with time but I still feel sad just thinking about him. Hilary.

★

For nearly twenty years I ran a boarding house, a job which is akin to being a school matron only with adults who needed a temporary home. The tenants were a mixed bag and I am not saying it was all easy; some of the residents did not get on with others and there were occasional clashes of temperament, but most of the time it was a genuinely happy, buzzy place to be. All this stopped when I retired recently. It was a long time since I had lived alone and at first it was very strange. I am making a good but different life for myself, but the loss of having a role, and of being needed has taken some getting used to. Janice.

★

In the mid-1980s we bought a beautiful Victorian terraced house in the "up and coming" part of Peckham in South London. I knew it was "the" house the minute I walked in. It needed a lot of renovation work but we gradually got it to how we wanted it. Our son grew up in that home and we had some amazing parties there. After twenty years we bought an apartment on the south coast as my husband was offered a new job there. For about a year we had a lodger in Peckham, and we went back at weekends. When the lodger decided to leave, my husband didn't want the responsibility of letting the house out so I reluctantly agreed to sell it and buy a house in the country. I loved the old house and six years on I still regret selling it. My heart sinks whenever I see a similar house and I feel the loss of it deeply. Lindsay.

I feel sad when I see how my grandchildren are being brought up. They are showered with material gifts, they live in a lovely house but they do not seem to get the nurturing they need. Unsurprisingly, they have become manipulative in order to get some attention and their manners leave a lot to be desired. As they approach adolescence I feel it is such a loss of the young people they could be if they had had a more caring upbringing. Jim.

★

I miss the wonder of Christmas as I get older. As a child it used to be such a wonderfully exciting time in the year, and even when my children were young it was special. Now it seems so commercial, so full of stress, and each December I feel a sense of grief coming over me for what used to be and cannot, somehow, ever be recaptured. Jenny.

★

Up until my mid-thirties my relationship with my mother was one of the most important things in my life, so much so that it might have been quite threatening to my husband. She and I seemed to be on exactly the same wavelength and I was greatly influenced by her opinions. As I matured, however, I started to drift further away from her both intellectually and emotionally and I struggled to keep our relationship together and to find areas in common. I think this was very painful for her, and looking back I feel it might have been that I was so close that I was almost a clone and I needed to distance myself quite radically in order to establish a separate identity. Most people do this to a lesser degree as teenagers, but I was obviously a slow developer. Unfortunately our closeness never really re-established itself to the same degree, and I have felt the loss of our friendship in her remaining years before dementia took hold. Sally.

★

And lastly, in parting, an inspirational quote from *Heartbroken: A Memoir through Loss to Self Discovery* by Kristine Carlson (after the death of her husband, Richard Carlson):

"To live a full life you have to live all of it. I cannot cherry-pick life's blessings and beauty without also keeping my heart open to its pain and sorrow. … Learn to accept life as it is, not as you think it should be or as you want it to be. That is the true secret of living a happy, contented life."